The Well of Life

More Sermons for the Seasons of Faith

— DOUGLAS DALES —

Sacristy Press

Sacristy Press
PO Box 612, Durham, DH1 9HT

www.sacristy.co.uk

First published in 2023 by Sacristy Press, Durham

Copyright © Douglas Dales 2023
The moral rights of the author have been asserted.

All rights reserved, no part of this publication may be reproduced or transmitted in any form or by any means, electronic, mechanical photocopying, documentary, film or in any other format without prior written permission of the publisher.

Scripture quotations, unless otherwise stated, are from the New Revised Standard Version Bible: Anglicized Edition, copyright © 1989, 1995 National Council of the Churches of Christ in the United States of America. Used by permission. All rights reserved worldwide.

Every reasonable effort has been made to trace the copyright holders of material reproduced in this book, but if any have been inadvertently overlooked the publisher would be glad to hear from them.

Sacristy Limited, registered in England & Wales, number 7565667

British Library Cataloguing-in-Publication Data
A catalogue record for the book is available from the British Library

ISBN 978-1-78959-264-1

In grateful and affectionate memory of Sister Benedicta Ward SLG

Vera Ancilla Domini

*Jesus said, "The water that I shall give someone will become
a well of water within, springing up unto eternal life"
John 4:14*

Contents

Preface vii

Part 1. Preparation and Penitence 1
1. The Mystery of Baptism 3
2. In His Presence 6
3. Follow Me 10
4. Master Key 14
5. Mirror of Truth 17
6. Ladder of Ascent 21

Part 2. Sacred Times 25
7. Remembrance Day 27
8. The Queen's Accession 30
9. Holy Kiev 33
10. The Lord's Anointed 37
11. A Vocation for Life 40
12. King Dei Gratia 43
13. Christ the King 46

Part 3. The Word of the Lord 51
14. The Beauty of Creation 53
15. The Word of God 57
16. The First Sign 61
17. Lynched for a Sermon 64
18. The Cure of Souls 68
19. Breaking the Bonds 71
20. The Heart of the Matter 75
21. You are the Christ 79
22. Can These Dry Bones Live? 82

23. The Palm Sunday Psalm 85
24. Risen Indeed 89

Part 4. Belief and Thought 93
25. True Priesthood 95
26. Breaking Barriers 99
27. Faith Seeking Understanding 102
28. The Transfiguration 106
29. The Name of the Lord 110
30. The Spirit Within 114
31. The Communion of the Trinity 118

Part 5. Communion of Love 121
32. Christian Marriage 123
33. Children at the Heart of God's Kingdom 126
34. The Fruit of Love 130
35. Enfolded in Love 133
36. The Spirit of Prayer 136
37. Faith, Hope and Love in the Face of Death 141

Part 6. Contemplative Worship 145
38. Divine Ascent 147
39. The Spirit of the Eucharist 150
40. Receiving Holy Communion 154
41. The Bread of Life 157
42. Encountering Silence 160
43. The Mystery of Faith 164
44. Sursum Corda 167
45. The Mirror of the Annunciation 171
46. Why we have Faces 174

Part 7. A Cloud of Witnesses 177
47. The Prayer of Mary 179
48. Mary—Mother and Martyr 183
49. The Making of Saints 187
50. St Cuthbert 190

51. Belief without Sight 194
52. St Dunstan 198
53. Light from the Isles 202
54. St Benedict 206
55. St James the Apostle 210
56. Jesu Dulcis Memoria 214
57. Amor Vincit Omnia 217
58. Glory Transformed 222
59. The Song of Creation 225
60. A Martyr King 229

Preface

This collection of sermons is a companion to *The Spring of Hope* that was published by the Sacristy Press in 2021. It is ordered on a different principle, however, shadowing the shape of the Eucharist in its topical structure. Before preaching, I often consult the sermons of those who have preached before me: Leo the Great and Augustine, Gregory the Great and Bede, Bonaventure, and Gregory Palamas. Bible references are drawn either from the Revised Version or the Revised English Bible and psalms often from the Book of Common Prayer; but some finer points of translation for emphasis are my own. Sometimes the set readings are included at the head of specific sermons where appropriate.

The second section reflects some of the momentous events of 2022: the Queen's platinum jubilee; and the tragic outbreak of war in Eastern Europe. It also marks the death of our beloved Queen Elizabeth II, and the accession of His Majesty King Charles III.

I am grateful to my colleagues and faithful parishioners, whose sincere interest, questions, and observations enable effective preaching and clarity of thought in our eight rural parishes. The whole process of writing up sermons after preaching them *viva voce* was prompted initially, and well before any lockdowns, by our three adult children, Christopher, Gwendoline, and Basil, who wanted a record of their father's preaching, and to whom I remain very grateful for their affection, interest, and encouragement. This book also commemorates someone well-beloved, who was a true godmother and friend to us all.

Douglas Dales
All Saints 2022

PART 1

Preparation and Penitence

1

The Mystery of Baptism

A sermon for Epiphany

In the Eastern churches, Epiphany marks primarily the Baptism of Jesus in the river Jordan by John the Baptist. In Greece, for example, the Cross is plunged into water, while in Russia Christians plunge themselves into cold water! The juxtaposition of the Baptism with the Cross is highly significant.

All the Gospels begin with the Baptism of Jesus, marking the beginning of his ministry and his emergence into the public eye as a rabbi with a mission. The historical context for this event has been amplified during the last century by study of the Essenes, and by the discovery just after the end of the Second World War of the Dead Sea Scrolls. The Essenes were communities of devout Jews, disenchanted with the political compromises surrounding the Temple in Jerusalem and alienated by the Roman occupation of their country: they withdrew into monastic communities in the wilderness. The Dead Sea Scrolls are the records of a similar community, and they shed great light on Judaism at the time of Jesus. The language of the *Benedictus* and the *Magnificat*, for example, compares with some of the prayers and expectations of this devout community, who hid their precious scrolls in pots in dry desert caves to protect them during the upheavals of the Jewish rebellion against Roman rule in the middle of the first century AD. The Dead Sea Scrolls provide the oldest extant texts of parts of the Old Testament and are therefore of vital importance to both Jews and Christians.

John the Baptist is in many ways the historical anchor of the Gospel story. Jesus and some of his closest disciples were firstly followers of John, as the Fourth Gospel makes clear. What happened to John presaged the fate of Jesus himself. Their ethical teaching was very similar, and the murder of John was a catalyst in the ministry of Jesus himself. He paid tribute to the significance of John, describing him as the greatest of the prophets. The followers of John the Baptist constituted an important element in the formation of early Jewish Christianity. Today in Orthodox churches, the icon of John the Baptist, or the Forerunner, stands opposite that of the Blessed Virgin Mary, either side of the principal entrance through the iconostasis into the sanctuary and altar of the church.

The Greek word "Epiphany" means the shining forth of divine glory and light, as in the story of the Burning Bush in Exodus 3. St Paul says in 2 Corinthians 4:6: "God, who commanded light to shine in the beginning, has shone into our hearts the illuminating light of the knowledge of the glory of God in the face of Jesus Christ." This is really a key text for understanding the meaning of the Epiphany and therefore of the Baptism of Jesus. In the historical event of the Baptism, Jesus was revealed as God's Messiah—the "anointed one" filled with the Holy Spirit. This was a private experience shared only at the time by John the Baptist, though later revealed by him to some of his followers (John 1:29–34). The identity of Jesus as the Messiah was later confirmed at the Transfiguration to three of his closest disciples. Both events point forward to the death of Jesus on the Cross, in the case of the Transfiguration quite explicitly. For in his Baptism, Jesus took the plunge into a disordered creation in order to redeem humanity, lost in its sins and prey to evil. What kind of Messiah was he going to be? His identification with God's people was going to be complete, a road of suffering, humiliation and misunderstanding, of conflict, pain and rejection by many.

The Baptism of Jesus reveals something more. In the midst of a very precise historical situation, the nature of God himself began to be revealed in a way that has laid the basis for Christian belief in the Trinity. The voice of the Father acclaimed Jesus as his beloved Son, and the Holy Spirit descended on Jesus in a palpable form. What is revealed in the moment of his baptism therefore is something true about the inner nature of God. Jesus revealed as God's Son is eternally his Son, and the descent of the Holy Spirit upon him as a human being reveals the eternal communion between Father, Son and Holy Spirit. The full implications of this belief took many years to unfold, but belief in the Trinity is what marks out Christian monotheism as distinct and unique.

This is why Christians are baptized in the name of the Father, the Son and the Holy Spirit. Christian Baptism has its roots in the saving Baptism of Jesus: his descent into the waters of the earth consecrated water as life-giving, not only in terms of natural existence, but also as initiating human beings into the eternal life and love of God. In Baptism, a person is united to Christ in his death and in his risen life; their sins are forgiven and washed away: they are called to a life of following Christ by "living through dying". Baptism is the foundation of Christian life and of the Church's existence, even if like many foundations it can be taken for granted or even ignored. But in early Christianity, Baptism was the pre-eminent sacrament, the gateway to Holy Communion, and for many a harbinger of martyrdom too.

St Paul speaks about the light of God being poured into human hearts. What is the nature of the light that streams from the mystery of Epiphany? The historical event of the Baptism of Jesus, Christian belief in the Trinity, and Christian Baptism are linked together by one inner dynamic: the self-giving love of God, poured out into the world in creation and also in redemption. In Jesus, the Creator comes among human beings as their re-creator. The perfecting work of God cannot be prevented by human sin, nor can it be overcome by the darkness of evil. There can be no variation in the loving purpose of God and his light alone gives life. To stand with Christ in the waters of Baptism is to stand at the focal point of that outpouring of light and love, focused in the person of Jesus in his life, death and resurrection.

"For it is God, who said, 'Light shall shine out of darkness,' who has shone into our hearts the illumination of the knowledge of the glory of God in the face of Jesus Christ." This is why in Christian worship "we all with unveiled faces, beholding and reflecting as in a mirror the glory of the Lord, are transformed into the same image from glory to glory, as from the Lord the Spirit" (2 Corinthians 4:6; 3:18). These words of St Paul, springing from his own spiritual experience, are the key to beginning to understand the mystery of the Epiphany, and also the hidden meaning of our own life in Christ, which is rooted in and determined by our own Baptism.

2

In His Presence

A sermon for Advent

The Latin word *adventus* means "drawing near" or "arrival", and it translates, not entirely perfectly, the Greek word in the New Testament *parousia*. This word conveys the significance of the opening words of Jesus in the Gospel: "The Kingdom of God is at hand" (Mark 1:15). Early Christians sensed that in Jesus the purpose of God had drawn very close to them, and that as they worshipped they could sense Christ's risen presence in the midst of the Church. We proclaim this today in our acclamation of the mystery of faith during the consecrating prayer of the Eucharist: "Christ has died, Christ is risen, Christ will come again." These words encapsulate the mystery of Advent. How may we approach it, and what is the spirit of Advent?

Early in the fifth century, St Augustine of Hippo composed his great work *The City of God* in response to widespread upheaval in the Roman world, epitomized by the sack of Rome in 410. This crisis prompted the withdrawal of Roman rule from Britain at that time. In his book, Augustine expounded a Christian view of human history that would exercise a great influence throughout the Middle Ages in the West. At the end of his book, he concludes with these famous words about heaven being the determining goal of Christian life: "In resting we shall see; and in seeing we shall love; and in loving we shall praise, in the end that is no end." For Christians, therefore, the phrase "the end of the world" does not mean its destruction, but rather the fulfilment of God's purpose as revealed in Christ: the word "end" therefore means "goal"—in Greek, *telos*. For Augustine, these words signified his vision of heaven and of eternal life. But they also provide a profound framework for us to enter into the mystery of Advent.

In resting

Christians are commanded to stop and stand still in contemplation and worship, and to rest in the presence of the Lord. "Be still and know that I am God" (Psalm 46:10). They are to build their lives upon the rock that is Christ (Matthew 7:24), as "living stones" becoming integrated into the loving purpose of God (1 Peter 2:5). In the midst of the world's turmoil and uncertainty, Christians belong to a kingdom that cannot be shaken: "Let us therefore have grace and thankfulness to offer worship that is well pleasing to God with due reverence and awe: for our God is a consuming fire" (Hebrews 12:28–9). Advent recalls us to the foundation of our faith and life: the reality of Christ, risen from the dead, and present at the heart of the Church. Our stability and certainty are found only in him. "Thus says the Lord God, the Holy One of Israel: in returning and rest shall you be saved, and in quietness and in confidence shall be your strength" (Isaiah 30:15).

In resting we see

Just as it is hard to focus a camera on a bucking deck, or when distracted by others, so it is hard to see and to hear the word of Christ without due concentration and attention. Do we cultivate this seriously, and do we know where we stand spiritually? The key to following Jesus is regular contemplation of the Gospels. His life, his teaching and his suffering reveal to us the truth about God, and also the truth about human nature, including our own. Christ is like a lens, and the closer that we come to him the more truly we shall see him; and the closer he will be able to come to us, with a transforming effect on our hearts and lives. "I see what you mean." Is it not odd that we link hearing and sight in this way? But it is true, of course, and we have to pray each day that by hearing the word of Jesus we may come to see what he means, and to sense the kind of person that he is.

In seeing we love

Christianity is not an abstract philosophy, nor simply a moral code; nor is it a religious cult. It is a living and loving relationship with the risen Christ. He came into the world to seek and to save human beings, by restoring them to a true relationship with God. We relate to God through him, and we discover that God is the *Philanthropos*—the true lover of humanity, and of each individual person who is made in his image and likeness. This is at the heart of the Gospel; and the reality of the love of God in Jesus Christ should govern the ethos of the Christian Church. Life is given to us so that we may develop a deep relationship of love towards God. Time is given to us to enable us to receive the transforming grace of his love for us by the indwelling of the Holy Spirit.

In loving we praise

Human beings are designed for the worship of God, and much mischief is abroad in the world because of the disordered use of this unique capacity. The word "worship" is about what we most truly value, to what or to whom we give true worth. St Augustine said in his *Confessions*: "God has made us for himself and our hearts are restless until they find their rest in him." This was Augustine's own experience, and he was the first to articulate it in this way. In the swirl of our preparations for Christmas, and in the midst of mounting anxiety across the world, Christians must stand firm in their worship of God and in ordering their priorities accordingly: we must always seek him with our whole heart.

In the Eucharist, the mystery of Advent is set forth for us each week: as Augustine also said, "On the altar, Christians see set before them that which they are called to become." This ancient service is the focus of the Church's existence, because the worship that we offer here participates in something deeper and eternal. "Therefore, with angels and archangels and all the company of heaven, we laud and magnify Thy glorious Name, evermore praising Thee, and saying: Holy! Holy! Holy! Lord God of hosts; heaven and earth are full of Thy glory: glory be to Thee, O Lord most high." The fullest picture of the worship of heaven and of the reality of the *Parousia* is found in the book of Revelation. As we proclaim these mysterious words, however, we also say, "Blessed is he who comes in the Name of the Lord; Hosanna in the highest!" We greet the risen Christ of the Gospels as we follow his steps all the way to the Cross.

In the end, we shall discover the truth affirmed by St Paul: "Who shall separate us from the love of Christ? . . . I am persuaded that nothing shall be able to separate us from the love of God, which is in Christ Jesus our Lord" (Romans 8:35–9). Jesus himself said: "Lo, I am with you always and forever, even to the consummation of the present age" (Matthew 28:20). Elsewhere he also said: "Heaven and earth will pass away, but my words will never pass away" (Luke 21:33). Advent recalls us to the fundamental truth that "there is salvation in no-one else, nor is there any other Name under heaven that is given among human beings by which we must be saved" (Acts 4:12). Let us therefore make the words of the Jesus Prayer our own personal, daily and loving response to Christ: "Lord Jesus Christ, Son of the Living God, have mercy upon me, a sinner."

3

Follow Me

A sermon for Petertide

Luke 9:51–62

The key word in this Gospel is "steadfast", which describes the single-minded determination of Jesus to depart from Galilee and to journey to Jerusalem, where his presence would pose a terrible challenge to the religious authorities, as well as alarm to his followers. What follows in this Gospel text indicates what it means for Christians to follow Jesus in a similar steadfast manner.

What might deter or distract us from so doing? When Jesus and his disciples were rejected by some Samaritan villagers because they were Jewish pilgrims, an ugly attitude of hatred reared its head in two of his closest followers, James and John. All the hurt and ethnic antagonism that poisoned Jewish-Samaritan relationships came to the fore, provoking them to call down fire from heaven to punish those who rejected Jesus as Messiah. His response and his rebuke began to change their attitudes at a deep level, however, which is why they remembered this moment. For, as St Paul later declared, "In Christ there can be neither Jew nor Greek, slave nor free, male nor female, for all are one in him" (Galatians 3:28). What attitudes of snobbery or racism lurk deep in our hearts? Christians have to be on their guard against such socially conditioned attitudes and values, which can mould young lives from the earliest days. What example is being given to our children?

The three sayings of Jesus that follow could be misconstrued as rejection of family and social commitments. But we know that Jesus was unequivocal in his commendation of stable marriage and the proper care of children. What was he challenging here?

It is vital to understand that their society was so close-knit that most individuals did not feel free to make radical choices about their lives. Yet some did, following John the Baptist and Jesus out into the desert and living on the margins of settled society. The desire for a permanent home is a natural human desire. But some Christians today, notably clergy and members of religious communities, still make the deliberate choice to follow Jesus at the expense of owning their own home for a long time, if at all. This cuts against the grain of a property-owning society such as ours, but it is a choice that should be respected and adequately supported, and never taken for granted. There is a cost to such Christian discipleship that is worth remembering at Petertide, when ordinations often take place.

Burial of the dead is a human and Christian duty. Yet there are times when following Jesus creates distance from family, being perceived as some kind of rejection of what is expected. The extreme nature of the words of Jesus "to leave the dead to bury their own dead" seems very harsh and, taken at face value, seriously wrong. What he is challenging, however, is the ease with which any of us can use family, friendships and social commitments, legitimate in themselves, to side-step following Jesus single-mindedly. Our first loyalty is always to him as the Lord of our lives. Sadly, many clergy and religious do not have the support of their families for the path that they have chosen. Such Christian vocation can entail real personal sacrifice and they need our prayers and friendship.

The third statement of Jesus also challenged the centripetal force of family and village life then, which clung on to individuals in a society where there was no social welfare support, and where, from a young age, children were often obliged to assume the livelihood of their parents for all to survive. The challenge of Jesus applies to everyone, then and now: for we accept today that artists, musicians and athletes, for example, have to be utterly single-minded and undistracted in order to excel. Such unwavering determination was and is the hallmark of Christian discipleship and holiness, and the radical nature of such Christian commitment is enshrined in monastic life. This offered an alternative choice of lifestyle in ancient and medieval society, which was respected and valued as such, and is still strong in Eastern Christianity. For clergy and religious in the West today, however, it is often too easy to lose heart and not to stay the course of a vocation freely chosen to follow Christ. Encouragement and support in their so doing is a duty laid upon all Christians, and vocations to religious life and priestly ministry should be prayed for and nurtured.

This past week, our Church has commemorated three such individuals, who in their own way stepped out of line to follow Christ. On 22 June, St Alban is remembered as one of the very few named Christians from the time when Britain was part of the Roman Empire. He lived in Verulamium, north of London, and gave shelter to a fugitive Christian priest during a time of persecution. When the authorities arrived to arrest the priest, Alban, wearing his cloak as a disguise, took his place, to the surprise of the magistrates who had to try him. He stood firm as a new Christian and was beheaded on the hill outside the city, where the abbey cathedral of St Albans now stands.

On 23 June, we remember St Etheldreda, who died around the year AD 678. She was a princess from East Anglia who was obliged to marry the king of Northumbria. She refused to consummate the marriage and in due time became a nun, living on an island in the middle of the fens, where she created a small monastery. She too stepped out of the line of her royal duty, but after her death her body was found to be incorrupt, and miracles occurred at her tomb. Today, Ely Cathedral now reigns in all its beauty, visible from far across the fens.

On 24 June, the Church commemorates the birth of St John the Baptist, and in the story told in Luke's Gospel, the pressure of family life and expectations can be clearly seen. They wanted to name him Zachariah after his father, but his mother insisted that he was to be called John, which means "the Lord is gracious": for her as an elderly mother, he was her miracle child. His father concurred, and so the prophetic path of John the Baptist began, a path that would lead him out into the wilderness, away from his family, living an ascetic existence and challenging those around him, high and low, to repent. His vocation proved to be fearless and radical, setting a pattern by which that of Jesus himself would be measured; and many of his followers later became Christians.

The writer of the letter to the Hebrews expresses very well early Christian memory of the steadfastness of Jesus: "Seeing we also are surrounded by so great a cloud of witnesses, let us lay aside every encumbrance and the sin that so easily clings to us: instead, let us run with patience and perseverance the race that is set before us, looking unto Jesus, the author and perfecter of our faith; who for the joy that was set before him endured the Cross, despising its shame, and is now seated at the right hand of the throne of God" (Hebrews 12:1–2).

4

Master Key

A sermon for Lent

The timing of Lent 1 this year could not be more apposite with its Gospel of the temptations of Jesus (Luke 4:1–13; Matthew 4:1–11). In the Russian attack on Ukraine, the world has witnessed this week, in graphic and harrowing detail, exactly how succumbing to such temptations ends up. To value things more than people, and to regard the world as something to be grasped, if need be, by force, culminates in sweeping human beings aside with cruelty and contempt. There should be no doubt about the genocidal intention of this Russian assault on Ukraine. To be able to wield inordinate and absolute power is to become corrupted; and to seek to make a country great by brute force leads to indiscriminate killing, as happened on a vast scale in the twentieth century. To become deluded into some fantasy of lost glory and imperial sway may have its roots in a genuine sense of grievance, loss and paranoia, but its end result is tragedy for all involved, as dark fantasy collides with reality.

Many people have been shocked by witnessing naked evil at work on a premeditated scale. The story of the temptations of Jesus smokes out the deep purpose of evil, which is to destroy the world of God's creation by corrupting human beings, and setting them against each other, destroying God's image and likeness in each of his human children. The nature of evil is to tempt, to bully and to intimidate; to nurture the desire to dominate others, to possess them, deny them, and finally to destroy them. This pattern can be seen throughout human history. Evil seduces people by playing on human hurts and grievances, and pandering to perceived good and justifiable goals. Becoming addicted to such dark fantasies, however, as happened with Nazism and Communism, is to become trapped by nihilism, which is the compulsive need to be cruel and to destroy. This unleashes frightening dynamics which its perpetrators lose control of in the end. No-one should doubt the existence and purpose of evil. Pray therefore each day, in the words of Jesus himself: "Lead us not into temptation, but deliver us from evil" (Matthew 6:13).

Christ came into the world to destroy the works of the devil and to enable human beings once again to become willing and obedient children of God. The temptations of Jesus can be placed in their precise historical context. They shed a sharp light on the pressures upon him as God's Messiah, pressures that dogged every step of his life and ministry until his death on the Cross. What kind of Messiah was he called to be? He lived among an impoverished and occupied people, the victims of Roman brutality. When he fed five thousand people, Jesus came perilously close to fulfilling popular expectations of a militant leader, who would lead a revolution and improve their lot (John 6:15). Instead, he said that "the bread that I give is my flesh for the life of the world" (John 6:51). Many Jews at the time resented the collusion of the Temple authorities with the Roman power, and withdrew into the desert to seek a purer expression of their faith in readiness for the coming of God's kingdom. Both John the Baptist and Jesus himself emerged from such a milieu.

When Jesus challenged the corruption in the Temple in Jerusalem, he again came very close to fulfilling expectations that he would be a second Moses, a true teacher and prophet of Israel. But he would not become a charismatic leader with a hold over his followers: instead, he said to them, "you are my friends" (John 15:14). Confronting Pilate, Jesus asserted that his kingdom was not of this world, saying "you would have no power over me were it not given you from above" (John 18:36; 19:11). In the words of St Paul, "he did not cling to equality with God, but emptied himself... and was obedient even to death on the Cross" (Philippians 2:7–8). By his non-violent stance, Jesus disappointed more militant groups, including some of his own disciples who were Zealots. The terrorism of the Zealots almost overthrew Roman rule thirty years later, but it led to the fall of Jerusalem and the destruction of the Temple. The followers of Jesus, however, never took up arms when persecuted, either by the Jewish religious authorities or by the Roman state. Instead, they challenged the cult of the emperor as a delusion and paid for this with their lives as martyrs.

The account of the temptations of Jesus serves as a master key for understanding how Christianity engages with and transforms human reality. To each person comes the challenge: do you value things more than people? Do you seek to dominate, possess and bully others, at home or in the workplace? Are you in danger of being deluded and manipulated by false images promoted by advertising and in the media, by politics or religion; or by behaviour like addiction; or by pursuing crooked values to the detriment of others as well as of yourself? These are searching questions for Lent, but of vital importance to individuals and to society. We pray, "cleanse the thoughts of our hearts by the inspiration of your Holy Spirit" because we know that our wills are so easily susceptible to wrong choices in response to temptation. The most potent of God's gifts to human beings is the will. He cannot manipulate our choices, but he seeks our love freely given. Can we truly pray, "Thy kingdom come: Thy will be done"? Can we take to heart and make our own the prayer of Mary at the beginning of the Gospel story: "Behold, I am the servant of the Lord: may it be unto me according to your word" (Luke 1:38).

In Lent, let us follow again the course of the Lord's ministry by reading at least one Gospel carefully, noting the pressure that Jesus was under and the choices that he made. His life reveals to us the nature of God himself: he does not manipulate people nor seek to control their minds; he does not dominate, but seeks the willing and loving obedience of the human heart. For he cannot force us to be good and loving. Instead, as St Augustine said, "Proud [humanity] can only be saved by the humble God." The writer of the first letter of John was probably commenting on the memory of the temptations of Jesus and their significance when he said: "Love not the world, nor the things that are in the world. If someone loves the world, the love of the Father is not in them. For all that is in the world, the lust of the flesh, and the lust of the eyes, and the vain-glory of life, is not of the Father, but is of the world. This world will pass away with all its lusts; but a person who does the will of God abides forever" (1 John 2:16–17).

5

Mirror of Truth

Psalm 25:1–10

It is customary to begin Lent by thinking about the temptations of Jesus in the desert, as recorded in Matthew 4 and Luke 4, and alluded to in Mark 1. Early Christians drew great comfort from the fact that Jesus had been tempted as we all are—"but without sin" (Hebrews 2:18; 4:15). This made him approachable and empathetic, but it also set his example as one to be followed. In the Gospel accounts of his temptations, it is notable that Jesus rebuffed the devil not by argument but by the use of Scripture; more precisely by quoting from the Law of God in Deuteronomy and also Psalm 91. Early Christians came to treasure the psalms as windows into the mind and experience of Jesus himself, for whom they were a primary instrument of prayer, privately and in the synagogue. To this day, the regular use of the psalms in prayer unites Christians with Jews in their worship and rich spiritual inheritance.

In his commentary on Psalm 25, Augustine said that "Christ speaks, but in the person of the Church; for what is said has reference to Christian people when they turn towards God." Medieval copies of the psalms often have titles which indicate how a particular psalm could be related to some aspect of the life of Jesus, or alternatively to the experience of the apostles; or to vicissitudes within the life of the Church as the Body of Christ at prayer. What is notable about Psalm 25 is that it is constructed using the Hebrew alphabet as a framework for memory and meditation: each line begins with a new letter of the alphabet. For Christians, it makes a brilliant mirror for contemplating our own life in the light of the life and experience of Jesus as recorded in the Gospels.

> Unto thee, O Lord, do I lift up my soul:
> O my God, in thee have I trusted;
> let not mine enemies triumph over me!

The Gospels record how diligent Jesus was in his own prayers, often waking early at dawn to go to a remote place to pray. How should we pray? The first step of prayer is to turn towards God and offer to him our soul, the very heart of our life, as the first priority of each new day: as in the words of another psalm, "early and eagerly will I seek thee" (Psalm 63:1). The second element of prayer is relationship—"O my God"—and all relationships are built upon trust. Do we entrust each day to the Lord? If we do, we have nothing to fear from anyone. It is those who do wrong who have something to fear—the final judgement of God as revealed in Jesus. For he was betrayed by those who acted shamelessly, betraying his trust and that of God himself.

> Show me thy ways, O Lord, and teach me thy paths:
> Guide me in thy truth and teach me.
> For thou art the God of my salvation, and I wait upon thee all day long.

When Jesus was alone in the desert, he was contemplating exactly what kind of Messiah he would be: a magician, a megalomaniac, or a manipulator of human hearts and minds? His adversary was, and is, all those things; and there are plenty of examples of human beings seduced down such destructive paths. They are not the ways of God, however. Jesus said, "I am the way, the truth and the life" (John 14:6). This means that every time a psalm reflects upon the way of God, Christians can apply it to Christ himself. The question is whether we want to be shown the way back to God. Are we biddable as Christian disciples to listen and to learn, and is this a priority in our lives? Do we sense God throughout the whole day, or only when we remember to say our prayers? What kind of relationship is it, however, that only turns to someone as an afterthought or as a matter of occasional convenience?

> Remember me, O Lord, in thy tender mercy and lovingkindness,
> which have ever been of old:

> Remember not the sins of my youth, nor my many transgressions.
> According to thy loving kindness remember me
> > for thy goodness' sake, O Lord.

In prayer, we are called to remember God even as we ask him to remember us. Note that in these lines the word "remember" occurs three times. We are not to take God for granted. "Remember" is a plea of love and also of humility. It is a plea of sorrow and apology for the many ways in which we have sat light to the commandments of God and disobeyed him. The actual words of the psalm speak of the many acts of mercy and kindness that we receive from God all the time. The challenge of Lent is whether we leave his love for us unrequited. In the Garden of Gethsemane, we glimpse how the temptation to doubt God stalked Jesus to the bitter end. "Remember me, O Lord!" This hope was expressed in his dying prayers on the Cross.

> Good and upright is the Lord,
> > therefore will he instruct sinners in the way.
> The meek he will guide in judgement,
> > and only to the meek he teaches his way.

What Jesus revealed is the unshakeable goodness of God, and the depths of his love poured out for the salvation of human beings: for "God so loved the world that he gave his only Son, that whoever believes in him should not perish, but should have eternal life" (John 3:16). God can be relied upon completely as a truly loving heavenly Father. The question of Lent is whether he can rely on us. We have to recognize our own sinfulness each day, and to shed any illusions about how we appear to God: we should pray sincerely, "Cleanse the thoughts of our hearts." Only then can we be taught anything by God. Jesus is "the way" that we are called to follow, the person from whose example we should be learning each day by reading the Gospel regularly with our prayers. Meekness means being biddable, humble, attentive and loving. Jesus was this kind of person, and this is what made him such a brilliant teacher of his disciples and friends, as their memory of him recorded in the Gospels confirms. God's way of teaching is one of guidance, enabling us to arise, to stand up, and to follow in the way of Christ from our own volition and with growing understanding. Being a Christian is thus a life-long education in the way of God as revealed in Jesus, for God's way is the way of intelligent love.

> All the paths of the Lord are lovingkindness and truth:
> unto such as keep his covenant and his testimonies.

This is a wonderful promise to make our own this Lent. Each of us has our own path to follow, but all our paths lead to the Lord; and the closer we come to him, the closer we come to each other, and to all those saints and servants of Christ who have followed the same call. The rest of this psalm intimates the demands and costs of the path of Christ as it leads to the Cross. This promise reminds us that whatever happens, lovingkindness and truth are two sides of the same coin, being attributes of God and characteristics of the ministry and teaching of Jesus. Scripture serves to keep before us the covenant and the testimonies of God in both the Old and New Testaments. These were the foundations of the ministry and teaching of Jesus, as they are of the life of the Church itself. Lent is the season when we can make sure that the foundation of our own life is firmly laid upon the rock which is Christ.

6

Ladder of Ascent

Exodus 20:1–17

In the treasury of the ancient monastery of St Catherine at the foot of Mount Sinai, there is a splendid twelfth-century icon which shows monks ascending to heaven by a ladder. It relates to a treatise called *The Ladder of Divine Ascent* by St John Climacus, who was abbot of the monastery in the early seventh century. This book has remained one of the most important works of monastic spirituality ever since. If you look closely at the icon, however, some of the monks are falling off the ladder into the hands of demons. The ladder of divine ascent is an arduous one, and each year in Lent we are bidden to grab onto the next rung and not to fall off.

The Ten Commandments set out the basic steps on this ladder of spiritual ascent. The first thing to notice is that we have to go down in order to begin properly to go up. The story of Adam and Eve in Genesis 3 portrays vividly and starkly the downward path of every human being in history and of every human society. Start with the last commandment: covetousness. Is this not the root of all human sin? Desiring something that is not ours, like Eve contemplating the fruit on the forbidden tree in the Garden of Eden: "The fruit was so desirable and it would make her so wise." Her disobedience to God's commandment was her downfall, into which she then lured her husband. Our society's advertising is saturated by covetousness.

Notice that to do this she had to deceive herself, and the path to self-deception is doubting God's reality and his commandments. "Did God really say that you should not eat of any particular tree in this garden? . . . You will not die!" What died, however, was their relationship with God, who had put them on trust; for without trust there can be no relationship.

This was evident when challenged by God as they cowered among the bushes; they lied to him: "I was afraid and I hid myself." They both tried to shift the blame for what they had done. If they had confessed and said sorry, perhaps it could have been different. The root of human alienation is disobedience towards God.

Their act of theft reveals the way in which human beings treat God's created world. How would you feel if someone were left in your home while you were away, and they wrecked it and its garden? Yet this is what is happening as humans pillage the natural world, with dire consequences for us all. "Thou shalt not steal." Our whole framework of law exists to protect us from each other in this respect. Meanwhile theft continues at every level of society. The root of theft is covetousness and its instrument is deception by telling lies. It is valuing things more than people, and to their detriment.

The downward path of humanity hit bottom in the next generation. Cain envied his brother Abel. He deceived him and stole his life by deliberately murdering him. Then he tried to cover it up when challenged by God. By so doing he broke his parents' hearts. "Thou shalt do no murder." His conscience had pricked him even as he tried to offer sacrifice to God. For God is the one "to whom all hearts are open, all desires known, and from whom no secrets are hidden". Had he prayed for the cleansing of "the thoughts of his heart", it might have been so different. Instead, violence became endemic in human society from the beginning.

"Thou shalt not commit adultery." Notice that in the Garden of Eden, Adam and Eve became aware of the disorder that they had brought into their lives and their relationship with each other and with God, by the uneasy awareness of their sexuality and their sense of nakedness and exposure before God. Adultery in the Bible means anything that disrupts stable marriage through unfaithfulness. Marriage is the only place where human sexuality can be safely expressed, and marriage exists primarily so that children can be loved and brought up properly. The sins of these first parents were visited upon their children in terms of Cain's wayward behaviour, and as a result their family life was damaged beyond repair, and Cain became an exile. Jesus endorsed this commandment about adultery when he indicated that it is unfaithfulness that lies at the root of things. This is not only sexual unfaithfulness, but also violence and abuse in the home, either within a marriage or towards children. Jesus was most stern in his condemnation of such abuse.

The foot of this downward ladder is actually the foundation for the upward ladder, however. Human beings cannot evade God forever and their attempts to do so are no more than fig-leaves in the end. There is only one God to whom everyone is answerable, and his intention is to free human beings from the slavery to sin and evil that they have brought upon themselves in every generation. The crucial question in Lent is this: what and whom do you most value? Jesus commands us to love God with our entire being, and then to extend this love to everyone else. Whatever we value in place of God is in fact an idol—and empty too. For as St Augustine said, "God has made us for himself, and our hearts are empty and restless until they find their rest in him."

Taking God's Name in vain means not swearing by him and not perjuring ourselves in court. But at a deeper level it means valuing our relationship with him as the central living reality at the heart of all that we do, and as the foundation of our obedience to him. In the Garden of Eden, Adam and Eve showed contempt for their relationship with God by their actions, and this contempt for God stretches down all the ages of human life until it reaches its climax at the Cross of Christ. Yet "there is no other Name given under heaven by which we must be saved" (Acts 4:12). In Jesus, God became a human being to restore us to himself. How do we value the Name of the Lord—our relationship with him—in our prayers and in our lives?

Lent challenges us to review our use of time. Are we too busy to pray? Too busy doing what? The Sabbath principle is a precious legacy from the Jews, and it needs to be reinstated in our relentless consumer society. Going to church and receiving Holy Communion must be the priority on Sundays. Giving time to family and friends by hospitality and recreation constitutes a vital link in the chain of life and activity between the holidays. Making priority time regularly each day for our prayers is the most basic rung of the ladder upwards back to God.

The way of Jesus shows us the rungs of this ladder upwards quite clearly, beginning with his temptations in the desert. "Being in the form of God, he did not snatch at equality with God: but he emptied himself, assuming the form of a servant. . . . Being found in human form, he humbled himself even to death on the Cross. Wherefore God has highly exalted him, and given him the Name which is above every name" (Philippians 2:6-9).

In the Gospels, it is quite evident that Jesus was the target of envy. He was lied to when he was betrayed by a close friend. His dignity was stolen from him when he was tortured, and he was murdered in a cruel way, which exposed his naked vulnerability and trashed his humanity completely and deliberately. All human sinfulness came to a terrible focus in his suffering and death. Evil also revealed its deadly hand, ever seeking to destroy humanity that is made in God's image and likeness by killing the One who is the Image and Likeness of God himself in human form. Only the way of the Cross provides the secure ladder up and away from this tragic human plight. "Follow me!" says Jesus to each one of us this Lent, "for I am the Way, the Truth and Life, and no-one comes to the Father but through me" (John 14:6).

PART 2

Sacred Times

7

Remembrance Day

> When you go home, tell them of us and say
> For your tomorrow we gave our today.

These haunting words from the Kohima memorial place each generation in our country under a solemn obligation to remember with sorrow and gratitude the tragic loss of so many young lives during the Second World War. The United Kingdom and most of Western Europe owe their subsequent stability and prosperity to those who fought so hard to defend the liberty and integrity of these islands, and then to liberate parts of Europe from tyranny. This is at the heart of Remembrance Sunday each year, and its commemoration has captured the imagination and commitment of a rising generation. But around this focal point are various other circles of remembrance. So, what else has to be remembered?

Firstly, that the Second World War was part of a thirty-year conflict with a twenty-year truce. Its roots lay in the bitter conflict of the First World War, in which so many were slaughtered on all sides. This had its roots in the Franco-Prussian war of 1870. This in turn arose out of the fears kindled by Napoleon's attempt to impose French domination across Europe, to the detriment of England, threatening invasion. Those facing Napoleon felt the same vulnerability as was later felt in 1940, because the liberty and integrity of this country was at stake.

Secondly, that the brunt of suffering in both world wars was in fact borne by the Russians. Their key role is often overlooked completely on Remembrance Day, but it should not be; and this omission still causes resentment. In the Second World War the very survival of their nation was at stake, and their casualty rate was ten times that of the Western allies. The scale of suffering on the Eastern front in both wars was appalling, and it contributed greatly to the rise of Communism, and to its persistence during the long years of the Cold War.

Thirdly, that civilian losses in both world wars, due to conflict but also to economic blockade, and compounded by the scourge of the Spanish flu pandemic, were so great that no European society emerged unscathed and unchanged. The severe trauma of 1914–20 gave impetus to the rise of Communism and then of Nazism. The economic disruption and rampant inflation contributed to the rise of vicious anti-Semitism. The price of war was indeed catastrophically high. The impact of these two wars was also global, leading to great instability and suffering in many parts of the world as Western empires collapsed, especially after 1945.

Fourthly, Remembrance Day is an occasion to remember all the unquiet dead—the many victims of dictatorships, deportations, genocide and evil concentration camps. These ghastly phenomena stretched on long after the end of the war in 1945 and persist today. Millions of lives were destroyed by Nazism and under Communism in Russia, China and Cambodia. History may well judge the twentieth century to be another Dark Age; and it casts its shadow over our own time, as human rights are abused, and Christians are persecuted in so many parts of the world today.

Finally, from the bitter conflict of the Second World War arose the technology of mass destruction, which culminated in the creation and use of atomic weapons to destroy cities. The shadow of this amoral development remains, and its fundamental cynicism calls into question all civilized and Christian values. The scale of the modern arms trade and the diversion of scientific and economic resources to sustain it are often overlooked. The ruthlessness of terrorism derives part of its driving force from this moral crisis at the heart of modern human society.

Remembrance Sunday obliges us therefore to consider seriously all that is at stake in our country and in the world today: the reality and value of individual freedom of thought, worship and expression; the rule of law, internally and internationally; the right to education and not indoctrination; the stability, character, values and integrity of our own country. Also, the need for international diplomacy and mediation of disputes; the recognition that grinding poverty is socially undermining wherever it is found; the realization that limited war must only be a last resort in self-defence, when all else has failed.

Christians approach Remembrance Day with a further perspective, because it brings into sharp focus the reality of evil in the world, which preys on human weakness and aggravates resentments that lead to conflict. "Deliver us from evil"—the words are those of Jesus in the Lord's Prayer, who was himself destroyed in an environment of hatred, occupation, racial resentment, violence and fear. But evil can only act when humans succumb to its malign influence. No-one looking at the events of the last century can doubt the reality and aims of evil, seeking the destruction of human beings, who are made in the image and likeness of God.

Every Christian prayer, and every celebration of the Eucharist, is a warding off of evil, a safeguarding of human hearts. It is putting love in where love is not; and Christians believe that such costly intercession is the only power in the world that can withstand and reverse evil. "Christians stand by God in his hour of grieving"—words of Dietrich Bonhoeffer, who was murdered by the Nazis in 1945 for his resistance to their tyranny. This is because Christians know that the Cross of Christ is the place where evil collides with the loving purpose of God as revealed in Jesus Christ. Remembrance Sunday therefore poses a profound challenge to us all, as we hear the words of Jesus himself: "Do this in remembrance of me."

8

The Queen's Accession

6 February 2022

We meet today to give thanks to God for the example and service of Her Majesty the Queen to the life of this country and to the Commonwealth. It is for her a unique moment of public celebration and private sadness, as it recalls the death of the person, King George VI, whose example has always guided her in all that she has given to us as our monarch; and our thoughts and hearts go out to her today in our prayers. It is a moment also to give thanks for those who have always closely supported her: the late Queen Mother and Prince Philip in particular, as well as others of her family, and especially the Prince of Wales at the present time. For hers has been for so many years until recently a strong marriage in the service of others, and this has been a source of profound strength to Queen Elizabeth in all that she has accomplished. To meet the Queen is to experience her sincerity and kindness, but also her dignity and steel: of her it may well be said, in words drawn from the Bible, "Thy gentleness has made me great."

As heir to the most ancient institution of this country, as Queen of England, our sovereign is the trustee of a unique monarchy, fashioned long ago in Anglo-Saxon times by the Christian Church. For over a thousand years, the rulers of England have sworn to uphold justice, to rule according to law, and to maintain the integrity and freedom of the Church. It is this principle of accountability that is one of the cornerstones of our constitution and our way of life. It is the principle that underlies all the manifestations of parliamentary government that take their origin from this country.

Queen Elizabeth has always believed that her duty is to all the people of her country without any social partiality, "for better, for worse, for richer, for poorer, in sickness and in health, until death us do part". This covenant rests upon a profound understanding of the example of Christ, the King of Kings, who came "not to be served but to serve". Each year on Maundy Thursday, the sovereign enacts this truth in a succession of cathedrals throughout the land. Compassionate service is the guiding principle of her inner life as a Christian as well as the root of her manifest sincerity.

Shorn today of all executive power, the monarch has become the embodiment of moral authority that underpins everything but that is beyond politics. The Queen demonstrates the life-giving nature of such authority expressed in a dedicated person; and her strength lies in her constancy through thick and thin, in times of public favour and in the face of mockery from various quarters. It is no mean feat to be beyond reproach and to stand fast through so many decades of relentless social change. Courtesy, kindness, duty and principle—these qualities outlast all the fads and foibles thrown up by such a restless society.

The Queen's great ministry has been to encourage the caring and charitable initiatives for which this country is widely and justly renowned. The capacity of the Queen to bring cheer and support to so many organizations in all types of communities is remarkable and invaluable. Without all that goes on in local, and often hidden, ways in our country, our common life would be vastly poorer, our international reputation would be dimmer, and many lives of ordinary people and those afflicted in various ways would be held back and neglected. Under her leadership, we demonstrate that we do care for those in need, and we will do something about this at every level, at home and also abroad. This is a great ethos to have nurtured as a queen among her subjects in the United Kingdom and also throughout the Commonwealth.

It has also been the determination of the Queen that has prevented our country from becoming too inward-looking. It was very difficult to steer the morale and sense of purpose of Britain as it emerged from the wreckage of the Second World War, the consequent loss of the Empire, and of our leading role in the world. She has insisted on keeping alive and strengthening the life of the Commonwealth, of which she is also the

Queen, often in the face of indifference and cynicism at home. Her farsightedness and patience have kept alive many relationships that might otherwise have atrophied, especially while Britain linked its fortunes to the European Union. She has especially encouraged work among young people, something that is very close to her heart. She stands today as one of the most respected people in the world: powerless, but also powerful, by virtue of her integrity, dedication and example.

The sovereign of England is also the Head of the Church of England, a duty that the Queen regards with the utmost seriousness. She has demonstrated that this is no empty title by her attendance at the General Synod, the support that she has given to successive Archbishops of Canterbury, and by her own initiatives to build strong ecumenical relationships between the various churches in her dominions. This vision has extended to embrace those of other faiths as well, in the pursuit of common values and social collaboration. For the Queen, as for many of her subjects, the twin pillars of the Authorized Version of the Bible and the *Book of Common Prayer* remain fundamental expressions of English Christianity. Her faithfulness in worship each week at church sets a fine example to us all.

When we think of Queen Elizabeth II, our Queen, the venerable titles that adorn our coins take on new meaning: "Queen by the Grace of God and Defender of the Faith". It is the authority of God and the example of Jesus that she would wish us to take to heart today, as the most fitting tribute to her role and achievement as the shepherd and servant of those whom she regards as God's people as well as her own. By her faith and example, Queen Elizabeth points beyond herself to something deeper and eternal: the love of God given to all human beings in the person of Jesus Christ. She has brought out of the royal treasure-house of the past "things old and new"; and for this she will always be remembered and cherished as a great queen, for whose happiness, health and wellbeing we will continue to pray today and for many years to come: "God save the Queen." Amen.

9
Holy Kiev

The Russian invasion of Ukraine is not only an affront to, and a flagrant denial of, Christian values: it is also an attack on Christianity itself. In the minds of some around Putin, including some leading Russian churchmen, it is partly a religiously inspired mission to retrieve and safeguard Kiev as the cradle of Russian Christianity. It is notable, and also tragic, that the Patriarch of Moscow has not only refrained from condemning this unprovoked aggression, but appears to bless it as a just cause. This will greatly damage the credibility of the Russian Church in the years to come, especially among a rising and younger generation in Russia and elsewhere.

It is true, of course, that Kiev is the cradle of Russian Christianity, a common inheritance treasured not only by Russian and Ukrainian Christians, but also by Orthodox and other Christians across the world. In this tragic conflict, Christians are now being pitted against each other, at least in military terms, and hatred is being rekindled, with bitter memories of how Stalin deliberately starved many millions of Ukrainians to death. Schism already exists between the Russian Orthodox Church and the Ecumenical Patriarch in Constantinople following his recognition of the identity of the Ukrainian Orthodox Church, and its right to be self-governing and independent of control from Moscow. Pursuit of historic-religious fantasy is at one level a crude justification for aggression; but at another level it is a dangerous intoxication that can only end in disaster, as it did for the Greeks in the aftermath of the First World War, who fantasized about regaining Constantinople, or the Serbs, who wished to regain Kosovo as an ancestral heartland and cradle of their faith. It is a misuse of history and a travesty of Christianity, raising false hopes and fears while justifying brutality.

The actual history of how Christianity came to become established in Kiev in the tenth century is well documented and important; and some buildings remain from this early period, most notably the beautiful cathedral of St Sophia, decorated with stunning mosaics by Greek artists, but also frescoed with paintings of Kievan court life by Russian artists. By some miracle, it has survived all the trauma that has afflicted the history of Kiev. The Monastery of the Caves, set high above the Dnieper river, was founded in the eleventh century by a Kievan layman, St Antony, who went to Mount Athos to become a monk. He was sent back to Kiev twice to kindle monastic life there, and he lived as a hermit in a cave above the river, where he attracted a following. The first monastery in Kiev was thus an outpost of the Holy Mountain of Athos.

His disciple, St Theodosius, created and formed the actual monastery above ground, where it remains to this day, surmounting two sets of caves where subsequently many holy men lived and died and are now buried. The *Life of St Theodosius* is one of the best early medieval saints' lives, portraying him as a humble monk, like St Francis of Assisi, who was nonetheless capable of standing up to, and gaining the respect of, the ruler of Kiev, Jaroslav, who supported the growth of the monastery. Nestor, his biographer, says of him:

> Theodosius was respected, not because of his fine clothes or rich estates, but for his radiant life and purity of spirit; and also, for his teachings, which were fired with the inspiration of the Holy Spirit. To him, the goatskin and hair-shirt were more precious than any king's purple robe; and he was proud to wear them as a monk.

The subsequent history of the monastery is carefully recorded in the earliest chronicle of Russian history. Many other monasteries and bishops sprang from the Kievan Pechersk Lavra, which became and still remains the motherhouse of Russian and Ukrainian monastic life.

Kiev itself became a prosperous medieval kingdom, being originally founded by Vikings and Slavs, and capitalizing on the trade that flowed along the Dnieper river, with close links to Byzantium, from where Christianity came formally to Kiev during the reign of Prince Vladimir.

He married a princess from there and was baptized along with many of his people in the Dnieper river by Kiev in 988. After his death, conflict arose among his successors. Russians remember and treasure the martyrdom of the princes Boris and Gleb, who were murdered by their own brother, but refused as Christians to use armed resistance to protect themselves.

Kiev had close links of marriage and trade with kingdoms in Western Europe, and some from the English royal family took refuge there after their defeat at the Battle of Hastings in 1066. In 1240, however, Kiev was overthrown by Mongol invasion from the eastern steppes and the Slav population came increasingly under alien domination for more than two hundred years, until the princes of Moscow began the fightback. Thereafter, Kiev was seldom free from foreign rule until finally being incorporated into the Russian empire of the czars.

Does this history matter, and does it provide a gleam of hope in the midst of the darkness of the current conflict? It surely demonstrates the truth that historical fact is stronger than myth, and that Christianity finds expression in actual historical situations from which later generations can learn much. Humility, accountability, charity, prayer, compassion, determination, education, non-violence—these were the Christ-like qualities that created Christianity in Kiev in the beginning, as they created Christianity in England as well. In every generation, they act like salt, as a corrective and challenge to the false values of sinful humanity. In Kiev, as in Rome, their reality may still be sensed, hidden behind the carapace and wreckage of history. For Kiev, like Rome, is a holy city for all Christians. But they are not qualities that can be appropriated by conquest or domination, religious or political; nor should they be distanced by sentimental idolization of saints; nor by fantasies about remote periods of Christian history as some kind of lost golden age.

On my first visit to Kiev in 1989, we were made very welcome and given the freedom to explore the city for a while. I was astounded by St Sophia Cathedral, which was the first Byzantine church I had ever visited. High in the beautiful apse is a commanding mosaic of Mary, the *Theotokos*, with her hands uplifted in prayer. Later that day, I made my way alone by bus to the terrible monument at Babi Yar, which marks the area where thousands of Jews and others were murdered in a ravine by the Nazis. It is surmounted by the figure of another mother, with her hands tied behind her back, unable to protect her little child, who sits on her lap. Two mothers—two martyrs to the suffering of their own children. It is terrible to witness this tragedy being repeated in the lines of families now fleeing Ukraine.

Kiev has often been a place where, amidst great trauma, darkness has collided with the light of Christ. Let us pray for and alongside all those in that holy city and elsewhere in Ukraine, that in the present darkness the light of Christ, crucified and risen, may yet shine forth and make all things new—for Russians and Ukrainians alike. In the words of Dietrich Bonhoeffer, written while in prison in Berlin in 1944: "Christians stand by God in his hour of grieving." Let us commend Russia and Ukraine and all their people to the intercession of the Holy Mother of God and of the founding saints of holy Kiev—St Antony and St Theodosius.

10

The Lord's Anointed

A sermon for Pentecost and the Platinum Jubilee of Queen Elizabeth II

"God is Spirit: and they who worship him must worship in spirit and in truth" (John 4:24). These words of Jesus endorse the widespread human spiritual experience, evident in many religions of the world. The sense that God is invisible but real; that there is a capacity in human beings that enables them to worship him; that such worship must be rooted in moral integrity and truthfulness; and that nothing is more damaging than worship misapplied to material objects or illusions, which is described in the Old Testament as idolatry. Plato also challenged this disastrous distortion of human thinking and belief among the Greeks of his day.

In the Old Testament, the Holy Spirit has a dynamic if elusive role, from the inception of creation to the inspiration of the prophets and the anointing of kings. In later Jewish belief, the Spirit was closely associated with divine Wisdom; and this rich tradition lies behind the language of the New Testament. What makes the New Testament teaching about the Holy Spirit so distinctive, however, is the way in which, through the person of Jesus, the Holy Spirit is perceived to be a divine person, someone to be received in a personal way. Jesus said: "When he the Spirit of Truth comes, he will guide you into all truth" (John 16:13); "You know him for he abides with you and will be in you" (John 14:17); "If a person loves me, he will keep my word; and *we* will come to him and dwell with him" (John 14:23). These are remarkable words, and it is the gift of the Holy Spirit through Jesus Christ that is celebrated at the feast of Pentecost.

When Jesus appeared to his disciples after his resurrection, he showed them his hands and side, still bearing the marks of his suffering, saying,

37

"Peace be with you: as the Father has sent me, so I send you ... receive the Holy Spirit" (John 20:20-2). Earlier, the evangelist observed that "the Spirit was not yet given [in this way] because Jesus was not yet glorified" (John 7:39). The outpouring of water and blood from the dead body of Jesus on the Cross came to signify the outpouring of the Holy Spirit (John 19:34). "It is the Spirit that bears witness to this because the Spirit is truth. For there are three that bear witness: the Spirit, the water, and the blood; and these three agree in one" (1 John 5:6–8). The gift of the Holy Spirit comes to us only through the Cross of Christ: his presence is sacrificial as well as sanctifying.

Christians believe that human beings are made in the image and likeness of God, and St Paul taught that each human body and person is designed and destined to become a sanctuary of the Holy Spirit (1 Corinthians 6:19). This belief is the foundation of Christian ethics: the unique value of each human person, and especially of each human child; the sense of accountability to God for the life that we lead and how we treat our bodies, and by extension our physical environment also; sensitivity to the dignity, worth and mystery of other people; and Christian marriage as the unique context in which children can be nurtured within the indwelling love of God that is already at work in their parents. Every time a person is baptized or confirmed, this truth is affirmed: "God has called you by name and made you his own: confirm, O Lord, your servant with your Holy Spirit."

The challenge of Pentecost is whether we are living up to the promises that we made at Baptism and Confirmation: to turn to Christ; to repent of our sins; to renounce evil. Also, to say our prayers each day, and to seek the light of the Holy Spirit as we read the Bible, ever seeking the face of Jesus in the Gospels. As we come to Holy Communion, we are to worship in spirit and in truth if we are to sense the presence of Christ in the sacrament, and perhaps even to discern the fiery descent of the Spirit upon the gifts of bread and wine. To worship in spirit and in truth means to worship within the loving communion of the Spirit and the Truth, which is Christ. This is something deeply personal and mysterious, as well as something shared in communion with other Christians, who are united with us in prayer and worship. "Behold, I stand at the door and knock: if anyone hears my voice and opens the door, I will come in and eat with him and he with me" (Revelation 3:20). Do we hear the voice of Jesus to us? Do we sense the quiet presence of the Holy Spirit?

At Baptism, Confirmation and Ordination, oil of anointing is often used to signify the embrace of the Holy Spirit, his healing presence and enabling love. To anoint a person in this sacramental way, and especially when they are sick, is to affirm their unique worth to God who created them, to Christ who redeemed them, and to the Holy Spirit who sanctifies them. It was with this in mind that in the eighth century, in France and in England, monarchs were first anointed by the Church. Initially this gave legitimacy to their rule as "the Lord's anointed", lifting it above crude tribal loyalties and the blood of battle for supremacy, and guarding them against assassination. It also meant, however, that Christian rulers were to be measured by the kingship of Christ and the law of the Bible; and in the tenth century in England, the wise men kneeling before the child Jesus came to be portrayed as crowned monarchs offering their crowns to Christ the King of Kings. By such means, the crucial principle of moral accountability and rule under law was gradually instilled by the bishops of the Church.

The English Coronation Order was composed in the tenth century by St Dunstan for the imperial coronation of King Edgar at Bath in 973. It incorporated elements already in use on both sides of the Channel, and although there have been subsequent revisions, in essence it remains the same today, which makes it unique and remarkable. It is notable that before the monarch is anointed, he or she must swear a solemn oath to rule according to law, to uphold the liberty of the Church, and to administer justice impartially. The anointing itself is a very private and hidden moment in the service, regarded as an enhanced form of Confirmation in order to fulfil a solemn vocation. Both the prayers used before and after the actual anointing were created in the tenth century, perhaps by St Dunstan himself. What is striking about the second prayer after the anointing is that it commits the ruler to an intimate and immediate relationship with Christ himself, to whom the prayer is addressed.

The quiet and patient faithfulness of Queen Elizabeth II embodies the truth contained in these ancient prayers, whose ethos has lain at the heart of Christian kingship in England throughout ten centuries. Her example and faithfulness can guide our own commitment to become partakers of the Holy Spirit, and so to follow in the footsteps of Jesus Christ our Lord.

11

A Vocation for Life

A sermon to mark the death of Queen Elizabeth II

We heard the sad news of the passing of our beloved Queen while we were with a community of Poor Clares in Lovere in Italy, to whom I was giving a meditation to mark the Nativity of the Blessed Virgin Mary on 8 September. I said to the nuns, when they told us the news, that Queen Elizabeth demonstrated the fruitfulness of a lifetime's Christian vocation. She believed that God had called her to rule as his servant; and this sense of personal vocation gave her direction, strength and purpose through all the vicissitudes of her long reign. Indeed, to judge by the spontaneous outpouring of love and devotion towards her by so many people across the United Kingdom, the Commonwealth and the world, she may come to be regarded as a royal saint, not least because of her gift of making people feel loved and valued wherever she went, which sprang from deep Christian belief and prayer and a generous heart.

The passing of the Queen challenges each one of us about our own vocation as Christians. She was bound by her life vows, taken at the Coronation in 1953. Priests, monks and nuns are also bound by life vows. There have been moments when the Queen's example has steadied and supported my own sense of vocation and direction as a priest. All Christians have a vocation, however, for each of us is called by Jesus Christ—"Follow me." At Baptism we turn to Christ in order to follow him, and at Confirmation we hear the moving words: "God has called you by name, and made you his own: confirm, O Lord, your servant with your Holy Spirit." For Jesus said, "I am the Way, the Truth and the Life: and no-one comes to the Father but by me."

Vocation implies being addressed by God and responding accordingly. God calls us to himself because he loves us and he has a purpose for our life. It seemed highly appropriate that the Queen should die on the day when the Church remembers the birth of the Virgin Mary. When she was born, no-one knew that she would become the mother of our Lord. When Princess Elizabeth was born, no-one knew that she would ever become Queen, let alone reign for so long and in such a wonderful way. But God knew—and both responded to his call. The prayer of Mary enshrines the essence of all Christian vocation: "Behold, I am the servant of the Lord: may it be unto me according to your word" (Luke 1:38). Can we make her prayer our own?

Christian marriage is also a vocation, a free and binding commitment for life to love and serve another person "for better, for worse; for richer, for poorer; in sickness and in health; until death us do part". This commitment derives its strength from God's commitment to us, his covenant of faithful love, given to us in the person of Jesus Christ. For as St Paul said, "I am persuaded that there is nothing that can separate us from the love of God in Jesus Christ our Lord" (Romans 8:39). With God's help, a Christian marriage can provide an environment in which children sense the faithfulness and love of God for them. Vocation finds its truest expression in example set, and this is what gives life and support to others in the family, and beyond. We celebrate and give thanks today for the life-long Christian example set by Queen Elizabeth.

It was strange and moving to watch from afar, half-way up a mountain in Italy overlooking a beautiful lake, as events unfolded at home. It seemed strikingly appropriate that as the Queen's body was laid in state in Westminster Hall, the Cross of Westminster should be raised at her head on the very day when the Church marks the feast of the Holy Cross on 14 September. This is because there is no true Christian vocation without cost. We do not know the sacrifices that the Queen had to make in order to pursue the narrow and demanding path of her reign. Archbishop Michael Ramsey once said that Christian ministry should be "joyful because sacrificial, and sacrificial because joyful". Many have testified to the loving cheerfulness of Queen Elizabeth, which flowed from her own following of Jesus Christ.

Jesus had his own vocation as God's Son, as the Messiah and Redeemer of his people. His mother Mary never expected to see her own son tortured to death on a cross. Yet his dying words—"Father, forgive them for they know not what they do"—culminated in words that echoed her own—"Father, into your hands I commit my spirit." His vocation was put to the supreme test in the Garden of Gethsemane, when he prayed, "Father, not my will but your will be done." We echo these words every time we say the Lord's Prayer, but do we know where they may lead us? For Jesus also said, "How narrow is the gate and how affected the way that leads to life, and how few are they who find it!"

Queen Elizabeth did find it, proving herself faithful in the midst of plenty, and following closely the example of Jesus himself to become for his sake the Shepherd and Servant of God's people. Today we pray that, with her, we too may hear the encouraging welcome of our Lord: "Well done, good and faithful servant: enter now into the joy of your Lord."

1 2

King Dei Gratia

A sermon to mark the Accession of King Charles III

The title *Dei Gratia*, which means "by the grace of God", and which appears on our coins, was first used to describe Charlemagne in the eighth century, and it was central to the Christian theology of monarchy developed at that time by Alcuin and others, which is now distilled in the English Coronation Order. A king anointed by the Church was in theory more protected against assassination or overthrow, being "the Lord's Anointed" like David or Solomon in the Old Testament. If his authority came from God, however, he was also accountable for how he ruled. It is striking that in the English Coronation Order, the monarch has to make a solemn promise of accountability before actually being crowned:

> In the Name of the Holy Trinity, I promise three things to the Christian people, my subjects: first, that God's Church and all Christian people within my dominions shall experience true peace; second, that I forbid robbery and all crime to every class of people; third, I promise and order laws based on justice and mercy, that the gracious and merciful God may forgive us all.

The various services marking the passing of our late beloved Queen have brought into sharp focus the Christian foundation of the United Kingdom, and no doubt this will be reiterated at the Coronation of King Charles III. It was notable that in his formal statements the new King declared his moral accountability towards the constitution and the Church of England. The Coronation Promise contains four vital principles that underpin a Christian country: the curbing of violence; the rule of law; impartial justice; freedom of worship, thought and speech.

Curbing endemic violence was the great challenge of medieval times. Very often this took the form of vendetta, which remains a problem in some parts of the world today. Creating a framework of compensation that would replace honour killing was one of the achievements of Anglo-Saxon law. Nonetheless, those centuries were violent and turbulent as Europe was upheaved by the inroads of the Vikings and others. It is easy to take a stable society like our own for granted, but the curbing of violence remains fundamental for human flourishing. Effective defence against enemies abroad and restraint of criminal elements within a country are the first duties of a government.

It is disturbing that across the Western world at present some people are sitting light to the fundamental principle of the rule of law. Christians believe that human law should have its foundation in the Law of God, and this was often invoked in medieval times. The divine command to love our neighbours as ourselves is the foundation for all law, as the law protects us from each other and regulates human behaviour in a way that is reasonable and accountable. Only a government that upholds and rules under the law is truly a government. Might is not right, and Cain's cynical question "Am I my brother's keeper?" was repudiated by Jesus himself.

The rule of law is undermined if justice is administered in a partial or corrupt manner. Impartiality is the principle that affirms the equal value of each person, whoever they are. But justice is also seriously undermined by social injustice, and the Bible is frank about the reality of this. In the parable of the Rich Man and Lazarus, Jesus highlighted the shocking gap in his day between rich and poor, the arrogance of the ruling class and its heartlessness. It is little wonder that some dictatorships have banned the Bible as a dangerous influence, for it contains an explicit challenge to all forms of despotism. In the Old Testament, for example, the prophet Samuel warned the people of the hazards of electing a king who would lord it over them, and later prophets were not sparing in their condemnation of corruption.

In England, from the beginning the link between the Crown and the Church has been close and influential. The Coronation Order was modelled on the consecration of bishops, and the establishment of the

Church of England has its roots deep in the Middle Ages; it was not simply an expedient arising from the Reformation and the breach with the papacy. The title "Defender of the Faith" is ironic inasmuch as it was granted by the pope to Henry VIII as a Catholic monarch before his breach with Rome! But today, as the late Queen has indicated, it commits the monarch to uphold the Church of England in such a way that all other forms of Christianity are also affirmed. The monarch also has a duty to safeguard the right to worship by the various other religious traditions now present in the United Kingdom, and this respect was apparent at her funeral in Westminster Abbey.

Inherent within the right to freedom of worship is the right to freedom of thought and expression. This is under threat from certain quarters in universities and the media. Pressure to be "politically correct" inhibits freedom of thought and speech, and the Marxist origin of this conceit is not difficult to discern. The principal duty of Christians is "to speak the truth in love", and to let others do so too, for freedom of thought and expression is essential within Christianity itself. Only open communication and mutual respect can underpin toleration, and only "speaking the truth in love" can guard against incitement to violence and discrimination.

The passing of our beloved Queen, who was so committed to these principles, and the welcome accession of our new King, whose values are the same, is a moment for our country to take stock of its own foundations and inheritance. For in the words of St Paul, "what have you that you did not receive?" (1 Corinthians 4:7). Although the Coronation Promise was drawn up over a thousand years ago, it epitomizes what is still essential to sound government today, in this country and elsewhere. Its principles remain as vital now as then, and they have to be understood and defended, and never taken for granted.

13

Christ the King

John 18:33–8; Luke 22:24–7; John 13:1–5

It is one of the paradoxes of Christian history that the artistic representation of Christ has so often assumed that of a ruler. Early Roman portrayals of the crucifixion present Jesus as triumphant and serene in his death. Byzantine mosaics portray him in the splendour of court dress, as the heavenly ruler or *Pantokrator* of cosmic significance. In the cathedral of Hagia Sophia in Kiev, for example, the face of Christ looms down from the dome of that lovely early medieval church. But in the much later church of the Peter and Paul Fortress in St Petersburg, the front of the main altar is decorated by a portrait of Christ as a Russian czar! Throughout Christian history, whenever the Church has been in alliance with the state, this phenomenon has occurred, often to the extent of making Christ seem remote and austere as the heavenly Lord and Judge. No-one can read the Gospels without noting the irony of this.

When on trial before Pilate, Jesus was directly challenged by him as the Roman governor: "Are you actually the King of the Jews?" To which Jesus replied enigmatically: "My kingdom is not of this world, for if my kingdom were of this world, my servants would surely fight for it ... but my kingdom is not such." In the context of seething Jewish rebellion that was brewing at the time, a non-violent Messiah was a contradiction in terms. Pilate, baffled, went further: "Are you really a king?" He was clearly out of his depth. Jesus replied: "It is you who say this because I am indeed a king. I was born for this purpose, and I came into the world to bear witness to the truth. Everyone who is of the truth hears my voice." What did Pilate hear when he responded in such frustration with the bitter and cynical words, "What is truth?" What Jesus exposed was Pilate's complete powerlessness in the situation.

What is the truth about kingship and authority that the coming of Jesus reveals? This prayer for the sovereign in the *Book of Common Prayer* is a good starting point:

> O Lord our heavenly Father, high and mighty, King of kings, Lord of lords, the only Ruler of princes, who dost from Thy throne behold all the dwellers upon earth; most heartily we beseech Thee with Thy favour to behold our most gracious Sovereign Lady, Queen Elizabeth; and so replenish her with the grace of Thy Holy Spirit, that she may always incline to Thy will, and walk in Thy way.

This beautiful prayer says a great deal, and we know that the Queen takes her vocation very much to heart as a Christian. It places all human beings equally before the majesty and judgement of God; it is a profoundly inclusive and universal prayer. It places the sovereign, and by implication all who exercise authority under her, within the commanding vision of God, to whom all are accountable. It asserts that true rulership flows from divine authority, and that its exercise requires divine grace. It calls the sovereign and her subjects to active obedience to the will and commandments of God. It reminds all in authority that there stands over them a higher divine authority by which their conduct is measured, and to which they are accountable: this principle of accountability underpins law and government. At the Coronation, a solemn promise of accountability is required of the royal person before he or she can be crowned, and this has been so for over a thousand years since the tenth century.

Early Christian mission in this country and elsewhere in Europe had to depend on the consent, support and protection of local rulers. This resulted in a consistent attempt by bishops and others to interpret kingship in the light of Christ. In practical terms, it meant defining laws and making sure that the king and those under him were accountable, which was no easy task in such a turbulent and violent society. But the impact of this can be seen in how Bede portrays kings and queens in his

Ecclesiastical History, in the laws framed by Alfred the Great, and in the rich development of the theology of Christian kingship articulated by St Dunstan in the tenth century, which had an influence across northern Europe. In the background to this development stands the *Pastoral Rule* of St Gregory the Great, who as pope defined his ministry as that of being "the servant of the servants of Christ". In practical terms, the ethos of Christian authority was encapsulated in the *Rule of St Benedict*, which people like Bede and Dunstan took as their rule of life as monks, commending it to bishops, kings and queens.

A key text underpinning this vision of Christian authority is found in St Luke's Gospel. With consummate irony, Jesus debunked the false values of his disciples, who were busy quarrelling about their pecking order in the coming kingdom of God. "The kings of the Gentiles wield lordship over them, even calling themselves their benefactors." The Jewish people were under the heel of the Romans—some benefactors! Instead, those who follow Christ must understand that authority has been turned on its head to reveal its true life-giving character. "It shall not be so among yourselves: let the greater become as the younger, and the leader act as the servant of all. For who is normally greater, the one who reclines at table or the one who serves? Surely it is the one reclining! But I am in the midst of you as one who serves."

In John 13, Jesus demonstrated the deeper meaning of this when he washed his disciples' feet at the Last Supper. This action revealed a profound truth: for "Jesus knew that the Father had given all things into his hands, and that he came forth from God and was going to God. He arose from the meal, laid aside his outer garments, wrapped himself with a towel, and pouring water from a basin, he began to wash the feet of his disciples, wiping them with the towel." This Gospel story lies behind the age-old custom of the sovereign distributing Maundy money each year as recognition of the truth of the Gospel and the example of Jesus. For in the words of St Paul, "Christ emptied himself, taking the form of a servant" (Philippians 2:7).

It is not difficult to track this principle of divine accountability throughout many of the parables and actions of Jesus, and it applies to us all in our daily lives. He says to us directly: "Insofar as you showed compassion to the least of those who are my brothers and sisters, you did it to me" (Matthew 25:40). The principle of accountability is the true foundation of all authority and leadership, and it underpins the rule of law. It also separates genuine governments, that are answerable to those whom they serve, from corrupt dictatorships. The kingship and example of Christ remains the standard by which all of us are judged.

PART 3

The Word of the Lord

14

The Beauty of Creation

The significance of Genesis 1

Around five hundred years before the coming of Christ, serious questions were being asked about the nature of created reality among Greeks and Jews. Plato composed his *Timaeus* and Jewish priests composed the opening chapter of Genesis. Both texts marched together in later Jewish and Christian thought, and consideration of Genesis 1 has commanded the attention of many of the most brilliant theologians throughout Christian history; for example, Basil, Augustine and Bonaventure. Teaching the Christian faith has always reverted to this very important text, as have the endless questions of the young in every generation. How should we think about Genesis 1 today?

The first thing to note is that its salient features have been broadly confirmed by modern scientific research. The primacy of light is the most striking note in Genesis 1, as is the sense that life on earth exists in a protective bubble called a "firmament". Notable too is the sense of the long ages of life on earth before the coming of humanity, and the perception that life emerged originally from the sea. It is interesting too that a firm distinction is made between the cold-blooded creatures, including the birds, and the emergence of warm-blooded mammals. It is also significant that the emergence of human life is placed firmly among the mammals, from which we know that we have evolved. Finally, Genesis 1 places human life as the crown of creation, the culmination of a long and purposeful development, which puts human beings in a consciously responsible relationship towards the created world.

There is no inherent collision between Genesis 1 and the progress of scientific research, and it can be argued that this passage has been a

53

profound stimulus to asking questions about how the world was made and continues to exist. The important thing is not to confuse questions of "how" with questions of "why". Scientific thought can hardly answer the question of why the world was ever created. It may simply set the question aside as unanswerable, or regard the world as the product of random developments linked together. Genesis 1 remains as a powerful corrective to such a monocular vision of reality. The fact that human beings ask why the world is as it is remains highly significant. Thinking about this may help to correct some of the modern attitudes towards the creation that have caused the ecological crisis.

Of course, Genesis 1 has to be seen in its historical context as something rooted in Babylonian astronomy and cosmological reflection. Jewish thought was at the time highly influenced by its exposure to the great civilizations to the east in Mesopotamia and to the south in Egypt. It is when Genesis 1 and indeed much of the Old Testament is placed alongside literature arising from those milieus that its distinctive character and originality become clear. Throughout the Old Testament, there is eloquent reflection upon the significance of the created world; for example, in the book of Job, or in the Wisdom literature, or as here in Psalm 8: "When I consider your heavens, the work of your fingers, the moon and the stars which you have ordained: what is man that you are mindful of him, or the son of man that you should visit him? For you have made humanity a little lower than God, and have crowned human beings with glory and honour. You make them to have dominion over the works of your hands, and have put everything in subjection to them."

Close reading of Genesis 1 reveals much else. It has a poetic structure of seven "days", or epochs. Clearly this cannot mean the 24-hour day as such, since the creation of the sun and moon and stars is placed centrally in the sequence on "Day" Four. Why is this so? Probably because the two great civilizations of Babylon and Egypt in their different ways venerated the sun and moon as creative deities. The writer of the biblical account displaces this belief, pointing to the existence of a single creating God, who is distinct from his creation.

Another striking feature of Genesis 1 is the assertion that the creation of the world is the expression of the mind of God, quite literally his utterance: "God spoke..." It is also the object of his continuing attention:

"God saw . . . " The primacy of light is of profound importance, and not just for subsequent physics. Light has a moral and aesthetic force as well. It determines the character and purpose of the created world as the expression of the goodness and glory of God. "And God saw that it was very good . . . " The word in Hebrew, and also later in Greek, for "good" means beautiful, wonderful, perfect, life-giving, delightful. Genesis 1 is thus a great poem celebrating the inherent beauty and goodness of creation.

In their different ways and springing from different traditions, the opening chapters of Genesis are concerned with the origins of humanity, and in Chapter 3 specifically with the origin of human sinfulness. Note that in the creation of humanity in Chapter 1, God seems to speak among himself: "Let us make . . . " The existence of the Holy Spirit has already been intimated at the beginning of the text, "brooding" over the chaos in the beginning. Now human beings are to be created "in our image and after our likeness". So, "God created man in his own image, in the image of God he created him, male and female he created them." Note that the fullness of the image of God in humanity is expressed in male and female together—by implication, equally. For Jews and Christians, this text lies at the foundation of marriage, as is evident in the explicit teaching of Jesus. For Christians, the phrase "the image and likeness of God" takes on a deeper meaning when seen in the light of Christ, the Word of God and the true Image of God expressed in a human person. This lies at the foundation of the Christian belief in the Incarnation.

In what ways might human beings be created "in the image and likeness of God?" In a way, the answer is implicit in the composition of Genesis 1, with its preoccupation with order, purpose, beauty and goodness. Humans are distinguished by their moral sense, their capacity to love, to think, to create language, to transmit knowledge consciously over time and space; to become creative; to engage in scientific enquiry using mathematics; to express truth and beauty in art, and supremely in music. Genesis 1 has had as profound an impact on art as it has on science. Its challenge remains: how do we see the world, and ourselves in it?

One way of thinking about creation is to regard it as a beautiful musical instrument, designed from material elements for a spiritual purpose, to communicate the truth and glory of God to those with ears to hear and eyes to see. This presupposes that there are beings capable of such a response. To be made "in the image and likeness of God" implies some affinity with God, some capacity to respond to him with love and wonder, and also with intelligent obedience. God did not have to create the world as he has, nor place human beings within it: but he did so freely, *ex nihilo*, and that is what we believe as Christians.

The modern ecological crisis has its roots in human blindness to this truth, treating the world as if it exists simply as a resource to be exploited. Genesis 1 challenges each generation to think again about how it sees the world in which it is placed. We have to pray to the Holy Spirit, who is the Lord and giver of life, to "enable with perpetual light the dullness of our blinded sight".

There is a beach near St Davids in Wales where pre-Cambrian rocks can be seen that are probably seven hundred million years old. They comprise volcanic ash from long before there was any life on earth. Scattered across the beach lie pebbles of every colour—pink, green, yellow, blue as well as grey—a striking demonstration of the profound truth that beauty is anterior to life itself: for the life of the world springs from the beauty of God.

1 5

The Word of God

A sermon for Bible Sunday

Isaiah 55:1–11; Psalm 19:7–14; 2 Timothy 3:14–4:5; John 5:36–47

I remember a Bishop of Salisbury once asking a congregation how many of them actually read the Bible regularly, either daily, or at least once each week: he got an embarrassingly poor response. It is a tragedy that in a society where copies of the Bible are freely available it remains unread in so many Christian homes. This was not always the case, and indeed British culture was largely nurtured by familiarity with the Bible and its language. Ignorance of the Bible closes the door to any real appreciation of Christian art, music, history and architecture. The challenge of Bible Sunday is therefore to read the Bible intelligently and regularly, and to encourage children and young people to do so too. This is because Jews and Christians believe that the Bible contains the Word of God. It is the place where the mind of God engages with the hearts and minds of men and women. Its authority underpins Jewish and Christian belief, and the Bible plays a key role in worship in the synagogue and church.

How may we approach reading the Bible? Firstly, we have to have some idea of its long history. The Old Testament is the oldest thing that most people will ever handle inasmuch as parts of it go back to the end of the Stone Age. For example, the story of Abraham portrays someone moving from stone circle to stone circle, seeking God in the context of prehistoric religious practices. The history of the creation of Israel in the reign of David is recorded in a vivid and immediate way that describes tribal conflicts in the Bronze Age. Later parts of the Old Testament, and especially the Apocrypha, reveal the influence of Greek thought. For several centuries before the coming of Jesus the Jewish Scriptures were translated from Hebrew into Greek, creating the Septuagint, and their religion became bilingual. The laws in the Bible, mainly found in the first five books, which constitute the Torah of the Jews, may be compared with known laws elsewhere in the ancient Middle East. One way of thinking about the composition of the Old Testament is to compare it with a tell, which is a mound created by repeated human settlement over many centuries. It comprises many levels, some of which intersect those that went before or derive material from them. In some ways, the Old Testament is also rather like a complicated geological landscape that takes some careful understanding. Most of it was written in Hebrew and copied faithfully by hand by the Jews onto scrolls through many generations.

The Christian New Testament is rather simpler and much shorter in its historical development; but the study of it is limited by the fact that there are no draft forms of it to be examined, and comparisons with other types of literature at the time are few. Nonetheless something of how it came to be can be discerned within its contents. For example, Mark appears to be the earliest written Gospel, used carefully by Matthew and Luke. Luke's Gospel is paired with the Acts of the Apostles, which was written by the same careful author, who was also the first Christian historian. Some details in the Acts have been confirmed by archaeology. John's Gospel is unique in its structure and sheds valuable light on the inner drama of the story of Jesus, as well as conveying important historical details about his several visits to Jerusalem. Paul's letters form a distinct body of material, often revealing more about his missionary activities than can be known simply from the Acts; their autobiographical element is unprecedented. Other letters in the New Testament give a glimpse of some of the earliest Jewish Christian communities, while the book of Revelation is a momentous response to the vicious persecution of Christians by the Roman state under the emperors Nero and Domitian. Some light is also shed on the New Testament by the writings of the Apostolic Fathers, who wrote letters at the end of the first century AD which sometimes refer directly to material and events in the New Testament.

For Christians, the Gospels constitute the heart of the New Testament just as the Torah constitutes the heart of Scripture for the Jews. Indeed, one way of thinking about the whole Bible from a Christian point of view is to envisage a triptych, which is a three-fold panel of art often found behind an altar in a medieval church or in an art gallery. A Christmas triptych, for example, could comprise the nativity of Jesus as the central panel, with the shepherds on one side panel, and the wise men on the other. When Christians hear the Gospel, its meaning has to be supported by the Old Testament on the one hand, and interpreted by the rest of the New Testament on the other. Certainly, it is impossible to do justice to the New Testament without understanding its foundation in the Old Testament. For example, the Feeding of the Five Thousand only makes sense when seen against the backdrop of the Exodus story in which the people were fed by God in the desert. But its portrayal in the Gospels echoes the early Christian Eucharist.

Another and more dynamic way of thinking about the Gospels is to consider a drama on stage. Jesus and those around him are the principal figures, but no less important is the subtle background, rooted in the Old Testament and the beliefs and expectations of the Jews at the time. Even more subtle is the way in which the language of the Gospels conveys belief in the resurrection of Jesus. For example, in the story of the paralyzed man, the actual word of command used by Jesus, to "arise", is a word used of resurrection. This healing is an epitome of the whole work of Christ, who came to heal and rescue human beings from physical and spiritual death. By so doing, Jesus challenged many religious attitudes of the day that tended to stigmatize the chronically sick, or to regard them as unclean. In the end, Jesus paid the price for his actions and authority by being paralyzed on the Cross.

For Christians, the Bible contains the Word of God inasmuch as Jesus is the key to understanding its meaning, for he is the Word of God become a human being. This means that as Christians read the pages of the Old Testament, they place his teaching and his suffering like a filter over the text, drawing out from it a pattern of meaning hidden within it that only makes sense in the light of the death and resurrection of Jesus. Perhaps the most notable example of this is the Suffering Servant portrayed in Isaiah 53 and in Psalm 22, as Jesus himself pointed to this in his own teaching about why he had to die on the Cross. The rest of the New Testament is a testimony to the way in which the Spirit of the risen Jesus changed the lives of people and empowered the growth of the earliest

Christian churches. Paul's witness to what it means to be "in Christ" is what gives his writings their unique value and authority. His life as a devout Christian Jew became a crucible in which his faith was remade by the fire of the Holy Spirit. Indeed, the Acts of the Apostles is in some ways the Gospel of the Holy Spirit. From the New Testament, therefore, springs the whole spiritual tradition and experience of Christianity.

If you wish to be part of this tradition and to experience the transforming presence of the Spirit of Jesus in your life, you have to read the Bible regularly and prayerfully. Prayer, as well as informed thought, is crucial, as the Bible is a product of prayer and thought in equal measure. If you do not pray as you read the Bible, you will never understand its meaning or come to experience the mysterious manner in which God so often communicates with human beings who read it in this way. It is also important to remember that the Bible distils memory: it was written by hand to be read slowly and carefully, not rushed through. Its poetic character makes it more like a great and subtle piece of music. The fact that it comes to us in printed form is deceptive, and it is not like anything else that you may read. Each word and phrase can nourish the soul as its hidden beauty begins to reveal itself to you.

The Bible is the most precious thing in your home and in your life: so treasure it and read it alongside your prayers. Christians should read part of a Gospel each day so that they truly come to know the person of Jesus, and allow him to change their lives into a more loving and devout following of him. Pray before you read, and let the Holy Spirit lead you into all truth by speaking to you through the pages of the Bible. Come to Holy Communion duly prepared by carefully and prayerfully reading in advance the passages of the Bible set for that Sunday's service. Then pray as you sit down quietly in church: "Speak, Lord, for your servant is listening."

1 6

The First Sign

A sermon for Epiphany-tide

John 2:1–11

This is the only mention of the mother of Jesus in this Gospel, apart from her appearance at the crucifixion of Jesus. This story almost certainly sprang from a family memory of a significant moment when Jesus demonstrated that his ministry was not going to be held back or controlled by them. It can almost be read in the first person of Mary speaking: "We went to a friend's wedding—Jesus and some friends came too—they ran out of wine—I said to him . . . he said to me . . . I told them . . . they obeyed him . . . " The reply of Jesus to Mary, "woman", seems very abrupt in English translation; but in the original Greek, no rebuke was intended, as can be clearly seen in his compassionate words to her from the Cross (John 19:26). What it signified was that Mary had no claim on Jesus as his human mother in the exercise of his divine power. He acted of his own free will—it was a gracious response to human need, prompted by his mother's request. When people invoke the prayers of the Virgin Mary, they need to bear this in mind.

For the evangelist, this was the first of many signs revealing the divine glory of Jesus to those closest to him. He does not use the word "miracle", however, rather the word "sign". What is the significance of Jesus turning water into wine? It is interesting that early in St Mark's Gospel, Jesus asks whether the friends of a bridegroom would fast while he was with them; if he were to be taken away, they would certainly fast then: moreover, "new wine only goes into new wineskins!" (Mark 2:19–22). In the Old Testament, God is often described as the bridegroom of Israel: how faithful was Israel as God's bride? The "bridegroom" in the Gospels is thus a coded description of Jesus as God's Messiah, and some of his parables describe wedding feasts. In which case, this local wedding in Cana was a mirror of the deeper wedding between God and his people, as is any true marriage; thus, St Paul advised husbands to love their wives as Christ loved the Church (Ephesians 5:25). This is why mention is always made at a Christian wedding of Christ's presence at the wedding in Cana, affirming marriage as central to the life of God's kingdom according to the unequivocal teaching of Jesus himself (Mark 10:1-12).

"Whatsoever he says to you, do it." This is the message of the mother of Jesus to us all. It was the secret of her own life: "I am the servant of the Lord: may it be to me according to your word" (Luke 1:38). Their humble action in filling the water-pots to the brim with water enabled God to act in Jesus, just as the boy offering his picnic was the catalyst for the Feeding of the Five Thousand (John 6:9). As the water-pots were used for Jewish ritual purification, the transformation of their contents symbolized Jesus fulfilling the Law and the prophets. The true purpose of the Covenant was now revealed as transformed in him. In Greek, the phrase "draw out" is normally used of living water from a well. Jesus offers living water springing out of the heart of a person to transform their life (John 4:10f.).

"You have kept the good wine until now!" These words point beyond themselves to a deep truth about divine providence, for Jesus said to his mother, "My hour has not yet come." Mark's story also points forward to the Passion of Jesus, when the bridegroom would be taken away. For Christians it is this intimation that links this first sign of Jesus to the sacrament of the Eucharist: in the words of St Paul, "The cup of blessing that we bless, is it not a participation in the blood of Christ?" (1 Corinthians 10:16). In this sacrament, the wine is blessed by the words of Jesus, "This is my blood of the new covenant that is shed for you." It partakes of the mystery that it signifies—it becomes the blood of Christ, poured out for the redemption of human beings. The Eucharist is also an anticipation of the heavenly wedding when God will be fully united to his people in the one Body of Christ. We therefore pray at the offertory, "Fruit of the vine and work of human hands—may it become for us the cup of salvation."

The sacraments of Baptism and the Eucharist at the heart of the Church's life become the wellspring of the sacramental principle that should form and inform all Christian life. Water, bread and wine become the means by which God transforms our life into the divine life and likeness and love of Christ, by the power of the Holy Spirit. In this divine light and love, all our life takes on new meaning and significance. Meals become sacramental; prayers at meals should be a regular priority; hospitality is at the heart of the Church's life—"I was a stranger and you took me in" (Matthew 25:35; cf. Luke 24:29–30). Moreover, use of wine blessed in the Eucharist precludes its abuse. No Christian can waste food with a good conscience, nor remain indifferent to those who are poor and hungry, without their daily bread.

The sacramental principle extends further to embrace our engagement with the natural world. For if the world exists for the glory of God and as the supreme expression of his creative purpose, who are we to despoil and exploit it? If matter can by divine grace become God-bearing, then art and music can also express the hidden presence and glory of God. An icon, for example, participates in that which it signifies and becomes a worshipping bridge between human and divine reality. For it is only in God's light that we truly see light (Psalm 36:9)—the true light that comes into the world in the person of Jesus, the Word of God (John 1:9). Words too may express sacramental reality, and this is the meaning of the liturgy of the Church and the language of the Bible, which contains the Word of God: "This is my body that is given up for you." In this Gospel story, the evangelist has excelled in painting a word picture of memorable clarity, beauty and profundity that manifests the glory of God in the face of Jesus Christ. His disciples began to believe in him as a result of this experience. Do we also believe in him and sense his presence as we draw near to him in Holy Communion?

1 7

Lynched for a Sermon

Luke 4:14–30

Luke gives great prominence in his Gospel to this memory of the local reaction to a sermon that Jesus once preached in his home synagogue in Nazareth. There are briefer accounts of this bruising encounter in the Gospels of Matthew (13:54–8) and Mark (6:1–6). Jesus initially established a reputation as a well-educated and popular rabbi. Why did things go so disastrously wrong on this occasion? Part of it was clearly local jealousy and resentment, a crude expectation that he could be bidden to work miracles for those who knew him well. For the evangelist, however, this was the first rumble of trouble that would culminate in Jesus being rejected at the highest levels in Jerusalem and crucified by the hated Roman occupiers.

Luke does not record the actual content of the sermon that Jesus preached: only the key-text, and the subsequent hostile reaction to the implications of what Jesus was teaching. It is a good principle to read an entire text being alluded to in any New Testament passage, and this is no exception. Isaiah 61 is one of the most beautiful passages of hope. It speaks of God's people being given "a garland of joy for ashes and the oil of joy for their mourning." They were in exile at that time, and their holy city and its temple were in ruins. The prophet predicted a complete reversal of fortunes, as their oppressors would become their servants: "You shall eat the wealth of the nations." Instead of obscurity and persecution, Israel's standing in the world would be transformed. Through their covenant of marriage with the Lord, his people would enable divine "righteousness and praise to spring forth before all nations". How would this destiny be achieved? Did it really mean for "all nations"?

Luke highlighted the opening words of this heady vision, regarding them as setting the agenda for Jesus as the Messiah, as the rest of his Gospel would reveal. Jesus was the one anointed with the power of the Holy Spirit. His ministry would address the needs of the most vulnerable. His coming challenged everyone to embrace the presence of the Lord in the midst of his people, in fulfilment of Old Testament hope. His mission would reach far beyond Israel, however, to include the Gentiles, as Jesus must have made clear in his preaching on that fateful Sabbath day.

Perhaps some in the congregation at Nazareth reacted as they did because they expected something very different from the Messiah. Poverty was endemic in their society. They were under alien occupation and subject to arbitrary acts of cruelty by their own local ruler, Herod. Did they expect the Messiah to lead a revolt and to rescue those held captive or hostage? What would he do about those being tortured and killed as reprisals for Zealot terrorism against Roman rule? If God truly cared for his people, how could he stand by and not act?

The rest of the passage from Isaiah 61 held out an intoxicating vision of hope, which could be too easily interpreted in terms of fantasy and revenge, however. What sort of Messiah was Jesus going to be, and why would he be ready to relate to foreigners? In a situation of such brutality, the experience of being bullied was too easily projected onto despised groups, such as the Samaritans. When the foreigner represented Roman tyranny or alien Greek culture, the natural response of those oppressed was to retreat into themselves. Hence devout Jews would not eat with Gentiles, even though their religious and political rulers often cut deals with the Romans to their own benefit. This was the society that Jesus had to address and steer through, as the Gospels make clear. In the end, he inevitably disappointed and threatened many people.

Nonetheless, the passage highlighted by Luke, about which Jesus preached, does indeed set out the agenda of Jesus as the Messiah. He did care for the poor and identified with them, and his own family life was relatively poor. He could communicate with those on the margins of society, who came to him for help on many occasions. He was not afraid of touching lepers, and when he cured paralyzed people, Jesus addressed their inner sense of fear and guilt. To cure the blind was a pre-eminent sign of being the Messiah, recreating what had been lost, or perhaps never experienced. Many who were victims of social discrimination found forgiveness and new life as a result of his compassion. He appealed to Samaritans and to sympathetic Gentiles on many occasions, some of whom became his followers. He challenged the racial and religious exclusiveness and fears of his own people.

By so doing, Jesus broke barriers in a way which has inspired Christian social and medical outreach ever since. He certainly challenged fatalism at its root. But his actions also threatened the fragile framework of false security raised by a society so vulnerable to poverty and illness, and devoid of any effective medical care. Such deep and chronic fear was too easily projected onto others: "God is punishing you for your sins." "God does not care for you—you are condemned already." "Samaritans and Gentiles are unclean—do not associate with them." This is why so many of the miracles of Jesus provoked fear and hostility, as he challenged deeply held social attitudes and prejudices. Some people felt exposed by what he was doing, even as many ran after him, awestruck in their desperation and need. His was an explosive ministry indeed, and raising Lazarus from the dead just outside Jerusalem and at the time of Passover was the last straw, and led to his destruction (John 11).

As we read the Gospels, therefore, all this has to be borne in mind, and it is the genius of the evangelists to be able to convey some of this grim reality to us in the way that they do. They convey something else, however, that speaks directly to our own society with its remarkable medical care. Before we dismiss the fears of earlier generations, we need to acknowledge the way in which the recent pandemic has shaken our own sense of security, provoking many irrational reactions. We can be too easily lulled into false security of another kind. The miracles of Jesus still put the spotlight on the deepest needs and inner "dis-ease" of human beings.

When Jesus cures a leper, should we not allow him to address the spiritual leprosy of our sins, hidden away inside us and which deface our souls? When he cures a paralyzed person, does he not challenge those inner paralyses that we dare not admit but which represent traumatic wounds to our hearts and relationships? When he restores sight to the blind, should we not pray each day, "enable with perpetual light the dullness of our blinded sight"? When he welcomes the sinner and the outcast, do we accept his welcome of us if we repent and return to him? Are we not all his prodigal children? Do we want him to heal us and to change our lives? Will we return to him?

The Cross of Christ reveals the depths to which divine compassion stoops in order to rescue and redeem humanity, lost in its sins and false values. Every healing miracle of Jesus is an illuminating part of that process of divine remaking, just as it is also a foretaste of resurrection. It is a terrible fact that so deep a probe of divine light and love disturbs the darkness within us, provoking the hostility, evasion and fear that culminated in the rejection of Jesus on the Cross. Luke's loving Gospel of hope portrays the work of divine restoration by God, who in Jesus is making all things new.

1 8

The Cure of Souls

Mark 5:21-43

This remarkable double story of healings by Jesus is given great prominence in all three synoptic Gospels. It is also one of three independently attested stories of how Jesus raised individuals who had just died: the other occasions were the raising of a widow's son at Nain, recorded only in Luke's Gospel (Luke 7:11-17,22), and the raising of Lazarus, which assumes critical importance in the unfolding of John's Gospel (John 11:1-44). To raise the dead was an overwhelming sign of the Messiah, comparable with the actions of great prophets like Elijah and Elisha in the Old Testament. Hence the desire of Jesus to keep the thing quiet.

It is important also to note that in Mark and Luke, the girl's father is named as Jairus, the ruler of a local synagogue. Perhaps this was an event that laid the basis for an early Jewish Christian congregation there? Names cited as witnesses always indicate the primary nature of a Gospel tradition. In this case, Jesus also summoned those closest to him, Peter, James and John, to act as witnesses to this momentous event, just as they were to be witnesses to his Transfiguration on the mountain, and of his agony in the Garden of Gethsemane. The singular conjunction of these two dramatic healings was unlikely to have been invented, however, and the Gospel narrative in Mark conveys a sharp immediacy and clarity of collective memory.

Mark's account also conveys the stark panic of the double crisis confronting Jesus. Both Jairus and the unknown women can almost be heard speaking, if the Gospel narrative is put into the first person: "I begged him—my daughter is about to *die*!" . . . "I thought to myself that if

I could only just *touch* his robe I would be healed!" There is nothing more alarming, and sometimes traumatic, than for a priest to be confronted with a double urgent demand on time and attention: perhaps on the way to the hospital, for example, for an urgent visit, and stopped in mid-tracks by someone else in urgent need. Or five minutes only to listen to a complete stranger and make a suitable response with no chance of follow-up. Or not rushing past someone begging on a platform or pavement while hastening to an engagement, perhaps a funeral. If a priest wears the collar in public, this can easily happen, as there are no limits to the cure of souls.

When Jesus healed people, he set an example then and now. Firstly, he gave time to individuals. He was not afraid to talk openly with women in a society where this was not expected of rabbis. He was not fearful of ritual contamination by talking with, and being touched by, a woman with gynaecological problems, which rendered her a hidden outcast in her own society, unable to worship in the synagogue or temple, while her illness rendered her ritually unclean.

Jesus set an example also of giving full and empathetic attention to the individual person in need at that moment. He was not prepared to be treated as a magician; and, at the risk of considerable embarrassment to himself and to her, he obliged her to come out into the open and speak with him face to face. Her physical plight revealed her hopelessness in a society where medicine was often ineffectual and also expensive. Her inner need for healing and affirmation was no less real and urgent, as her religion and society condemned her plight. The words of Jesus conveyed his deep love for her as a person: "My daughter, your faith has made you well: go in peace now, and be completely free from your affliction." The words of Isaiah were being fulfilled: "Surely he has borne our griefs and carried our sorrows" (Isaiah 53:4). The empathy of Jesus was profound, as was his keen sensitivity to others around him, even in the press of a crowd and while responding to an emergency.

At the same time, such a public action by Jesus challenged and began to dismantle the primitive belief that women were inferior and even religiously unclean because of their menstrual cycle. This belief persists in some parts of the world today. By giving such attention to a dying child, Jesus also rebutted the inevitable fatalism of any human society without reliable medical care. This little girl mattered to him in a society where perhaps a third of children died before the age that she had reached. Confronted by the chilling and dismissive words, "Your daughter is dead—why trouble the rabbi any further?", Jesus commanded trust on the part of the parents, as well as of his closest friends. For in the New Testament, the word "faith" always means "active trust": and such trust rests upon a loving relationship with God as he comes to us in Jesus. Meanwhile, the professional mourners and others standing by mocked Jesus: for a rabbi to touch a dead body would render him ritually unclean, so why bother?

How Jesus acted in the home was also instructive. He safeguarded the privacy of the family and thus the dignity of the child. He took her by her hand, and the actual Aramaic words he spoke are only recorded in Mark's Gospel: "*Talitha cumi*"—"Little girl, wake up and get up!" Such compassion touches the heart of any parent, and their unique role was affirmed by the practical humanity of Jesus when he told them to give the child some food. They never forgot that moment.

In a way, this double story sums up the whole meaning of the Gospel, as Jesus the life-giver comes among human beings to liberate them from death, physical and spiritual. Both miracles are acts of resurrection, of healing and liberation; and both challenge and overturn the heartlessness and fear in human society, even as they affirm the unique value of each person and each child who is made in the image and likeness of God. One very practical reason for reading the Gospels regularly and attentively is to learn from Jesus how God actually deals with people, and to follow the example he set.

1 9

Breaking the Bonds

Mark 5:1–20

This striking story is told in all three synoptic Gospels, and its earliest form is undoubtedly in Mark's Gospel, where it is recounted from vivid memory. Its significance is profound, and challenging too. It marks the moment when the mission of Jesus as Messiah reached out beyond the confines of God's people, Israel, to embrace the needs of others—the Gentiles. The area where it occurred was called the Decapolis, which had been settled by a mixed population of Jews and Gentiles—hence the keeping of pigs, which Jews regarded as unclean. In the small world of the first disciples, this was breaking bounds, and in a dramatic way.

This encounter poses a challenge to every generation of Christians: the dilemma of chronic mental illness. In those days, there was no effective treatment, and conditions often ran out of control, as toxicity and trauma compounded suffering and induced paranoia. The tendency to draw back from such suffering, and for its victims to become social outcasts, was inevitable, as people always find mental illness threatening, hard to comprehend, and often impossible to deal with. This often remains true today, and it is the duty of the Christian Church to overcome indifference and hostility towards the mentally ill, to love them, and to champion their needs.

The deeper tragedy of the situation then was that amidst such ignorance evil preyed upon mental illness and took advantage of the inevitable fear and social ostracism. This man had become a monster, banished to the tombs among the ghosts, mutilating himself in his distress, a figure of horror. "No-one had been able to tame him", and his strength seemed superhuman and very dangerous: "he could not be bound." Yet when he saw Jesus, he ran towards him and worshipped him. This is highly significant, and it reveals the fact that however ill and confused a person may be, with mental illness or dementia, they remain a child of God. Their soul remains intact and its affinity with God, in whose image and likeness it is made, is not destroyed. This was the inner wellspring of his response to Jesus, who approached him like light arising in the darkness of his plight.

What is striking about Mark's Gospel is that it is only the demons who actually recognize the hidden divinity of Jesus. This is apparent from the beginning—for example, in the synagogue in Capernaum (Mark 1:24). Only the High Priest challenged Jesus directly about his identity in these terms (Mark 14:61). That evil in a person can recognize holiness in another, and recoil from it, is evident in many saints' lives, and also in the pastoral experience of priests today. Who is speaking to Jesus—evil within the person, or the person himself? What is notable in this story is that the ministry of deliverance was already underway from the moment the man approached Jesus.

To name evil is to command it and to identify its real and insidious character. The name "Legion" echoed and perhaps mocked the Roman occupation itself. It was a soubriquet but also an apt description. This encounter with Jesus exposed the depth and complexity of evil as it besets human beings, individually and socially. Its power is formidable as it twists human energies, fears, illness and ambitions to its own destructive ends. This is apparent today in the scale and barbarity of the war in Ukraine. For the purpose of evil is to deface and destroy human beings, made in the divine image, as part of its endless war upon God himself.

In their day, such infestations of evil were often locally perceived and identified, so the place needed liberating as well as the person. Many modern Christians find the wholesale destruction of the herd of pigs deeply offensive. But what this signified was the demonstrable scale and completeness of the deliverance. Indeed, today, if a home is to be exorcised, care has to be taken with domestic animals that can be easily alarmed: for however evil is conceived, its presence and reality can be palpable, fearful and disturbing. It also signifies the way in which the deep spiritual disorder within human nature impacts the order of creation, distorting and damaging it: alas, "the whole creation groans and travails in pain" (Romans 8:22).

This is why the local people reacted as they did. They could not handle the situation and found Jesus a threat to public order and their economic livelihood. Certainly, this action would have drawn the attention of the Roman occupiers to someone who could pose a problem. What the people actually encountered, however, when they came to Jesus was remarkable. The possessed man was "sitting, clothed and in his right mind". "Sitting", because his tormented soul was at rest in the presence of Jesus his Saviour. "Clothed", because he was restored to society as a child of God. "In his right mind", because he had been liberated from the malign manipulation of evil, which had twisted his mind so fearfully. One of the worst manifestations of the fall of humanity is the way in which evil gains entry into the human mind and can control it. The restoration of the human mind and will was central to the mission of Jesus, who commanded people to worship God "with all their mind" (Mark 12:30).

Naturally, the liberated person wanted to accompany Jesus and his disciples, who had shown true friendship to him. Instead, he was commanded by Jesus to go home and to tell all who would listen about his miraculous deliverance—about "the great things that the Lord has done for you, and how he has had mercy upon you". Normally, Jesus wanted his miracles kept hidden, though this was hardly likely in such a close-knit society. But in this case, the person became a missionary to his own people, a harbinger of the mission of the Church to the Gentiles. This raises the interesting question of how this story was remembered in such a detailed and vivid way that the other evangelists, Matthew and Luke, hardly alter its substance at all. Clearly, it made a great impact on the disciples of Jesus, and if the story is couched in terms of "we" rather than "they", this can be sensed—"we came to the other side of the sea (of Galilee) . . ." Another possibility is that the testimony of this person was the seed of an early Christian community in the Decapolis, a foundation story of how Jesus changed lives. It is very personal, reflecting the fact that someone so disturbed could nonetheless be capable of remembering vividly the turning-point of his life.

In the minds of the evangelists, this story was highly significant as demonstrating the truth of the Gospel, that Jesus is able to save to the uttermost those who turn to him, whoever they are, and whatever their plight. "For the Son of Man came to seek and to save the lost" (Luke 19:10) and to destroy the works of the devil. Holiness alone drives out evil, and this is why Christians are called to become "the salt of the earth" by their diligent prayers and fearless compassion.

2 0

The Heart of the Matter

Deuteronomy 4:1–2,6–9; Psalm 15; James 1:17–27; Mark 7:1–23

Whenever there is direct ethical teaching by Jesus in Mark's Gospel it is always highly significant, as this Gospel is not marked by so much teaching as in the Gospels of Luke and Matthew. This deliberate assault by Jesus on an obsession with ritual cleanness undermined much that is false in human life and religion. The tendency to turn rules into weapons of division and oppression is evident in so many social contexts, even today. In a religious context, this can lead either to discrimination towards outsiders, or to a false sense of self-righteousness towards God. In the time of Jesus, strict Jews would not even eat with Samaritans or Gentiles for fear of ritual contamination. The Pharisees were sticklers for keeping the finer points of the Law, which had become set about by a host of customary regulations and interpretations. The conversion of Paul, a Pharisee, reveals the great burden of expectation, guilt and fear that such legalism can create in a person's life. The temptation to revert to moral legalism has been evident quite often in Christian history, and it is a serious spiritual snare.

In this passage, Jesus exposed the hypocrisy that legalism can so easily induce. He challenged the ease with which some twisted the interpretation of the Law to unworthy ends. It seems that he may have been educated among Pharisees for a while, and certainly some of his early followers emerged from such circles. This is probably why his exposure of their hypocrisy was so damning—for them, but also for Jesus himself. "You depart from the commandment of God and cling to merely human traditions!" This stricture can apply as readily to parts of Church life today. The particular point at issue here was the ease with which dedicating wealth to the service of God could be used to evade fundamental moral duties towards the care of parents.

It would have shocked his Pharisaic hearers that Jesus appealed quite openly to the common sense of the ordinary people, thereby undermining their claim to a higher and more self-righteous morality. "There is nothing outside a person that by being consumed can defile a person morally. It is what proceeds from the heart of a person that defiles him or her." This destroyed the whole basis for discrimination between Jews, Samaritans and Gentiles in terms of eating together. The Christian Eucharist demonstrates this fundamental truth: for "in Christ there is neither Jew nor Greek, male nor female, slave nor free". This is why barriers to Holy Communion between Christians are so wrong, and why in the Anglican Church we do not maintain them.

In his explanation to his disciples, however, Jesus puts the emphasis where it belongs in the sight of God: in the human heart. "It is from the heart of a person that evil thoughts proceed." The list given by him is explicit, comprehensive and searching: "fornication, theft, envy, wickedness, deceit, lust, jealousy, anger, pride, folly". These all have their roots deep in the attitudes and false values of the human heart. They manifest profound disobedience towards God himself. It is the distinctive feature of the Bible that at every turn it is the heart of a person that is at stake as the key battleground where the love of God is either lost or won.

This can be seen in the other passages set for this Sunday. In Deuteronomy, the Lord commands his people to "take heed to yourself and keep your soul diligently, lest you forget the things that you have seen, and the memory of them departs from your heart all the days of your life; instead, make them known to your children and to your grandchildren". In Judaism and also in Christianity, memory in worship is a potent means of safeguarding the human heart for the love of God that is expressed by faithfulness to him. It is thus a shared memory that defines the People of God, most notably at Passover among the Jews, and in the Eucharist for Christians when Jesus says, "Do this in memory of me."

In Psalm 15, only a person "who speaks truth in the heart" may enter the tabernacle of God, and only someone who "walks uprightly and works righteousness" may dwell on his holy mountain. This psalm outlines the obligations of faithfulness to the Law of God in terms that echo the Ten Commandments, and which foreshadow the teaching of Jesus in the Gospels. In the letter of James, the ethical teaching is no less direct: "If anyone seems to be religious but cannot control his tongue while deceiving his own heart, that person's religion is a sham." This reminds us that it is the attitudes of our hearts that need correction, and that repentance means a complete change of mind. Only the indwelling love of Christ can achieve this within us, as we have no power of ourselves to change ourselves from this baneful inheritance of original sin. This is why we pray at the beginning of the Eucharist, "Cleanse the thoughts of our hearts by the inspiration of your Holy Spirit." This should be our daily prayer.

We need to pray also for discernment, so that we are not seduced by false values, or manipulated by those whose intentions are corrupt, even if they seem to be religious and devout: "Do not be deceived, for every good giving and every perfect blessing is from above, coming down from the Father of lights, with whom can be no variation, nor shadow of turning." The hallmark of the love of God is his faithfulness, expressed to the uttermost in the death of Jesus for us: his gifts are revealed in how they are given to us. The question is whether we will twist and turn out of his light and so become impervious to his self-giving to us. The question is also whether our lives can become consistent and faithful as embodiments of the Love of God. It is notable that those who applied double standards in the name of religion and engaged in hypocrisy were the hardest for Jesus to reach. He condemned their inconsistency and self-deception, and they in the end helped to plot his destruction. Jesus warned about discerning people by the fruits that their lives actually bear; and the fruits of the Spirit cannot be conjured out of pretence and acting.

But God is not mocked, and the Bible makes it utterly clear that it is by our hearts that we are judged in his presence, now and hereafter. Whether we like it or not, our hearts are always open to him: there is no hiding place. We know also that the proper healing and ordering of the human heart is the most difficult thing; and its disorder is the root of much misery, spiritually and psychologically, and also in terms of damage to human relationships. "Be doers of the word of God, and not hearers only, deluding yourselves." Do not look into the mirror which is the life and face of Jesus Christ and then turn away. For in Christ, who is the

Image and Likeness of God himself, is the image and likeness in which we were each made and to which we are called to return. "Someone who looks into the perfect law of liberty and continues to do so . . . shall be blessed in so doing." Jesus said in the Gospels, "by their fruits you will recognize them", as people whose religion is true because it is rooted and expressed in compassion, as "pure and undefiled before God our Father". Again and again, we must therefore pray: "Cleanse the thoughts of our hearts by the outpouring of your Holy Spirit."

2 1

You are the Christ

Mark 8:27–9:1

If the Transfiguration is the pivot of Mark's Gospel, this famous dialogue is no less central in its importance. It is recorded as such in the Gospels of Matthew and Luke (Matthew 16:13-28; Luke 9:18-27), and the moment of Peter's articulate recognition of Jesus as the Messiah—the Christ—is noted also in John's Gospel in a different context: "We believe and know that you are the Holy One of God" (John 6:69).

One way of interpreting the significance of this dialogue is to relate it back to the temptations of Jesus, which are not actually recorded in Mark's Gospel. In these temptations, in the fourth chapters of Matthew and Luke, Jesus was tempted to act as a magician and to win popular support by feeding the people. He came perilously close to this at the Feeding of the Five Thousand when they wanted to turn him into a king (John 6:15).

Jesus was also tempted to seek political power and to overthrow Roman rule. This was the eager expectation of many at the time, notably the Zealots, who anticipated the Messiah as a liberating ruler like King David of old, and acted accordingly with terrorist attacks on the Roman occupiers, which finally resulted in war and the fall of Jerusalem in AD 70.

Jesus was tempted to manipulate the minds of his hearers, acting as a charismatic and commanding prophet and teacher, taking the Temple establishment by storm and overthrowing a corrupt regime. This he came close to provoking by driving out the traders from the Temple precincts on two famous occasions. What kind of Messiah was he going to be, wherein lay his authority (Mark 11:28), and what popular pressures were upon him throughout his ministry? These fears haunted his critics in the Temple establishment and led to his downfall.

In this dialogue at Caesarea Philippi, the disciples of Jesus reported popular estimation of Jesus as a second Elijah figure, perhaps even John the Baptist returned from the dead, and certainly, a great prophet. Some of his disciples had been followers of John the Baptist before they joined Jesus, and this prophetic expectation runs throughout the Gospels (cf. Mark 11:27–33). It can be seen also in the writings of the Essenes and of the Jewish monastic community, whose scrolls were found in a cave by the Dead Sea. As Jesus hung dying on the Cross, the association with Elijah was raised once again—in mockery: "Let us see if Elijah will rescue him now!" (Mark 15:36).

Peter's profession of faith in Jesus as the Messiah—the Christ—brings to a climax the question never far from the surface in the first part of this Gospel: "Is this really the Messiah?" The reaction of Jesus in commanding secrecy and silence was to protect his position for as long as possible, not least from false expectations among his own disciples, as well as those of the wider public. Instead, the Gospel of Mark records here the first of three solemn predictions by Jesus of exactly what would happen to him in Jerusalem (cf. Mark 9:30–2; 10:32–4). The vocation of the Son of Man was to suffer many things: to be rejected by the Temple establishment, to be killed by the Roman occupiers, and then to rise again from the dead. What is striking in the Gospel is the way these predictions were so precisely remembered, even though at the time they could scarcely be clearly understood, let alone accepted.

Peter spoke again for them all when he protested that this fate could hardly happen to God's Messiah, let alone to their beloved master and friend. For as Paul said later, the crucifixion of the Messiah was blasphemy and a scandal to devout Jews, as well as being folly to Gentiles (1 Corinthians 1:23). Crucifixion was the most odious instrument of Roman rule. How could God's Chosen One become God's Cursed One? Sadly, Peter's voice was the voice of temptation, this time through the affections of a close friend: "Get behind me, Satan!" The critical issue during the temptations had been what kind of God would Jesus believe in and represent? What is the nature of God's power—over nature; over human nature; over the hearts and minds of human beings? In many ways each Gospel story and encounter provides part of the answer. The second part of Mark's Gospel addresses the question: "If Jesus truly is the Messiah, the Son of Man, why must he suffer and die?"

There follow some of the most astonishing words in the Gospels: "If anyone wants to come after me, let him deny himself and take up his cross and follow me." It is too easy for Christians to take the words "take up the cross" for granted. What could it have meant to his hearers, to the disciples and to others listening in at that moment in time? Such a striking saying of Jesus was remembered vividly, however, and not just on this occasion (cf. Matthew 10:38; Luke 14:27); and it has become the key symbol of Christian discipleship ever since. His exposition in this dialogue of the beginning of its meaning echoes the choices Jesus made in the desert during his own temptations, when he repudiated the path of power. "What would it profit someone to gain the whole world but to forfeit his soul?" This is the fundamental choice facing everyone when confronted by evil.

In every generation, disciples of Jesus have to follow him every step of the way to Calvary. The genius of the Gospel writers lies in their capacity to remember how they stumbled along this bitter path, only partially understanding what was going on, while remembering so sharply the words of Jesus at every turn. This is why close reading of the Gospel is the best preparation for Holy Week and Easter. For us to be ashamed of Jesus and what happened to him is to avert our gaze from the truth revealed in the Gospels—the truth about human nature in its dire need; the truth about evil; and supremely the truth about the nature of God's power and love expressed in the person of Jesus himself.

This dialogue concludes with a challenge and a promise, however. Some of those standing close to Jesus, including Peter himself, would glimpse his divine glory on the hidden mountain of Transfiguration. The coming of the kingdom of God "in power" would be fulfilled on the other hill of Calvary, near which lay the empty tomb—the gateway to the resurrection of Jesus, who would trample down death by his own death, and break the power of evil over human nature once and for all.

2 2

Can These Dry Bones Live?

Mark 12:18–27; Ezekiel 37:1–14; Psalm 16

One of the most striking things about the Gospels is the way in which they record that the disciples of Jesus remembered him predicting his resurrection without being at all sure what it might mean (Mark 9:9–10). The dialogue of Jesus with Martha at the tomb of Lazarus addressed belief in the resurrection directly in response to her belief that "he will rise again in the resurrection at the last day" (John 11:24). The raising of Lazarus demonstrated dramatically that resurrection was not simply to be placed at the end of human existence. Eternal life is a reality now because Jesus declared that "I am the resurrection and the life: a person who believes in me, even though he dies, yet shall he live" (John 11:25).

How did Jesus convey the significance of resurrection and eternal life? In Mark 12, there is a dialogue with some of his critics among the Sadducees, a priestly circle of theologians, who were sceptical about resurrection and who regarded the miracles in Scripture as belonging to a remote past. Later, Paul was able to exploit the controversy between Pharisees and Sadducees about this to his own benefit when on trial before the priests in Jerusalem: "The Sadducees say that there is no resurrection, nor angel, nor spirit" (Acts 23:8). It is not difficult to find such an attitude abroad in our own secular society and among some theologians.

In Mark 12, Jesus was posed a hypothetical question by some Sadducees about a woman who was married in succession to seven brothers, each of whom died so soon after the wedding that no children were born. "So, in the resurrection, whose wife will she be?" (Mark 12:23). The background to this mocking and heartless questioning lay in a moving story in the

Apocrypha about how Tobias, son of Tobit, received Sarah as his wife. She had been married to seven husbands, each of whom had died before the marriage was consummated. The servants blamed the girl, saying that she was cursed by evil, and their mockery drove her to the brink of suicide: "Already seven husbands of mine have died: what have I to live for now?" She was rescued from her despair, and Tobias from his fear of her as evil, by the angel Raphael (Tobit 3:7-17; 6:9-14). The critics of Jesus alluded to this story as a way of disparaging his teaching about resurrection.

The reply of Jesus to his critics in the Temple was forceful: "You do not understand the Scriptures, nor do you know the power of God" (Mark 12:24). His own teaching could not have been more explicit: "When people rise from the dead, they neither marry nor are given in marriage, but become as the angels are in heaven." He directed his learned critics back to the roots of Jewish belief, to the appearance of God to Moses at the Burning Bush below Sinai: "I am the God of Abraham, the God of Isaac, and the God of Jacob" (Exodus 3:6). The conclusion was clear therefore: "God is not the God of the dead but of the living: you are seriously mistaken" (Mark 12:27; cf. John 8:56). The raising of Lazarus in John's Gospel fulfilled words of Jesus spoken earlier, that "the hour has now struck when the dead will hear the voice of the Son of God, and those who hear him will live" (John 5:25). In the Gospels, there are three independently recorded occasions when Jesus, like Elijah and Elisha before him, raised a person who was dead. His raising of Lazarus, however, sealed his own death sentence.

In Ezekiel 37, the vision of the prophet provides a backdrop to Christian belief in resurrection as it emerged in the New Testament as a result of the resurrection of Jesus himself: "Can these dry bones live again?" The valley of dry bones is a graphic symbol of human hopelessness in the face of death; for what is the meaning of life itself if this is all that there is in the end? People go to great lengths in every society to bury this deep fear, to avoid death, and to sugar over the reality of dying. "Our bones are dried up and our hope is lost: we are completely cut off" (Ezekiel 37:11). The prophet was bidden to invoke the Spirit of God, who alone can recreate human beings. The miracle of resurrection is two-fold, because eternal life is only born by the inbreathing of the breath of God himself. "You will know that I am the Lord, when I open your graves and cause you to emerge from them; and I will put my Spirit within you and you will live" (Ezekiel 37:13–14). In John's Gospel, Jesus breathed upon his disciples with the words, "Receive the Holy Spirit" (John 20:22). The first Christians (Acts 2:25–8) found in Psalm 16 words that encapsulated their belief and hope in the light of the risen Jesus, and when confronted by the reality of death itself: for this prayer was the experience and testimony of Jesus himself.

2 3

The Palm Sunday Psalm

Psalm 118

When Jewish pilgrims came from far and wide to keep the Passover each year in Jerusalem, they would chant a number of set psalms of ascent as they solemnly approached the holy city, including Psalm 118. All four Gospels record that this psalm was indeed chanted as Jesus approached the city, mounted on a donkey. Jesus himself referred to it in one of his final confrontations with his critics in the Temple (Mark 12:10); and Peter referred to it in his first letter (1 Peter 2:7). Peter is also recorded as citing it in an early confrontation with the religious authorities in Jerusalem (Acts 4:11). Psalm 118 is therefore a very important clue to understanding the way in which the earliest Jewish Christians perceived the significance of Jesus as God's Messiah. The challenge that they faced was this: how could God's Chosen One become God's Cursed One? Crucifixion signified being utterly condemned, "for a person hanged on a tree is cursed by God" (Deuteronomy 21:22–3). This was why the Romans as the occupying power used it to humiliate the Jews. How would the words of Psalm 118 have related to the events surrounding Jesus that the followers of Jesus witnessed and remembered?

Psalm 118 looks back to all the mighty acts of deliverance by God experienced by the people of Israel since their exodus from genocide and slavery in Egypt. In the circumstances of their occupation by the Romans, its words were defiant—a protest song. Inasmuch as they anticipated the coming of the Messiah as a deliverer, chanting this psalm was more than a protest, it was a cry for liberation. Despite everything: "*Give thanks to the Lord, for he is good; for his mercy endures forever.*" The experience of the people then became personified in the experience and testimony of a representative individual, as it does also in the figure of the Suffering Servant in Isaiah 53. It is not difficult to see how the earliest Christians would hear these words as expressing the experience of Jesus himself:

> Out of my distress, I called upon the Lord:
> > he answered me and set me free.
> The Lord is on my side: I will not fear: what can men do to me?
> The Lord is alongside those who help me:
> > I shall see my desire upon those who hate me.

Jesus was walking into a political trap, engineered by his religious enemies in the Temple hierarchy. The shape of this entrapment was carefully recorded in all the Gospels as the crisis came to boiling point, and Jesus was betrayed and arrested. His silent stance before his accusers, both the High Priest and the Roman Governor, set an example of non-violent resistance that Christians never forgot.

> It is better to trust in the Lord than to put any trust in men.
> It is better to trust in the Lord than to have any confidence in princes.
> Foreign nations encircled me,
> > but in the Lord's name I will cut them off.

The deliberate calculation behind how Jesus was destroyed was evident at every turn. His critics tried to trip him up in his teaching and turn the people against him. He had to keep Passover in a secret safe house before experiencing the bitterness of betrayal by a close friend. His adversaries were terrified of him and accused him of blasphemy. They engineered his destruction by the Romans rather than by stoning in order to shift the blame, while at the same time discrediting any claim by Jesus to be the Messiah: for a crucified Messiah was a contradiction in terms and a scandal (cf. 1 Corinthians 1:23).

> You thrust deliberately and deeply so that I might utterly fall;
> > but the Lord helped me.
> I shall not die, but live: and declare the works of the Lord.

> The Lord has chastened me sorely,
>> but he has not given me over to death:
> You have answered me and become my salvation.
> Open to me the gates of righteousness:
>> I will enter them and give thanks unto the Lord.

The earliest Christians recognized in these words the mystery of the Passion: the deliberate malice of human beings doing the destructive work of evil itself against God; the suffering of Jesus as a sign of God's involvement in all that happened to him; and the unexpected mystery of the resurrection—"I shall not die but live." In the words of Paul, "God was in Christ reconciling the world unto himself" (2 Corinthians 5:19).

Psalm 118 also enabled them to come to terms with the tragedy of the rejection of Jesus by those who should have acclaimed and supported him—the hierarchy in the Temple in particular.

> The stone which the builders rejected
>> has become the principal cornerstone:
> This is the Lord's doing, and it is marvellous in our eyes.

Jesus cited these words as a warning to his critics at the end of his last parable in Jerusalem—the parable of the Vineyard (Mark 12:10–11). Peter cited it as vindication of early Christian belief in Jesus as God's Messiah, crucified by men, but now risen from the dead (Acts 4:10–11).

The pilgrims following Jesus on Palm Sunday as he entered the holy city of Jerusalem acclaimed him with words from this psalm: "*Blessed is he who comes in the Name of the Lord—Hosanna in the highest!*" Luke's Gospel says that they also acclaimed Jesus explicitly as a messianic king (Luke 19:38; cf. 13:35). No wonder that some Pharisees and others standing by urged him to silence his followers. This was being dangerously provocative, for at the previous Passover pilgrims from Galilee had been massacred by Roman forces who were garrisoning Jerusalem (Luke 13:1).

These words, *Benedictus*, have passed into the Christian liturgy: we say them in the middle of the consecrating prayer of the Eucharist, immediately after the *Sanctus*. For at each Sunday service of Holy Communion we commemorate the mystery of the Incarnation, and also of Easter itself—the Cross and the Resurrection of Jesus; and we sense his risen presence among us now in the breaking of bread.

> This is the day that the Lord has made: we will rejoice and be glad in it.
> Save us now, O Lord! We beseech you, send us prosperity.
> We bless you in the house of the Lord:
> > for the Lord is God, and he gives us light.
> Bind the sacrifice with cords, even to the horns of the altar.

The resurrection of Jesus holds open the door to the eighth day of God's new creation. The death of Jesus saves us from the clutches of evil and the contagion of sin: it delivers us to the healing and wholeness of eternal life in him. The hallmark of Christian worship is joyful thanksgiving for such a deliverance and such a promise, the abolition of all fear. In this divine light, we see the sacrificial nature of the suffering of Jesus, and bow before its mystery each time the Eucharist is celebrated. Then the closing words of this great psalm become our own heartfelt prayer.

> You are my God, and I will give you thanks.
> You are my God, and I will exalt you.
> Give thanks unto the Lord, for he is good;
> For his mercy endures for ever.

2 4

Risen Indeed

John 21; Acts 9:1–9; Revelation 1:9–18

The moving account of how the relationship between Peter and the risen Jesus was restored is even more remarkable for the way in which the fate of Peter was predicted by Jesus so clearly. To descend beneath the great basilica of St Peter's in Rome into the Scavi is not for the claustrophobic. But it leads right down to the necropolis in which the remains of Peter were first buried and later venerated by early Christians, on the edge of what was then the Vatican circus, where he had been cruelly and mockingly crucified upside down.

It is no less striking to hear in conjunction with this Gospel the story of the conversion of Paul on the road to Damascus, an event so important that it is recounted three times in the Acts of the Apostles and referred to by the apostle himself in his letter to the Corinthian church (1 Corinthians 15:8). The cost of his conversion was clearly spelled out to him by the Lord, and he too ended up in Rome, where he was beheaded. The fourth-century casket which contains his remains may be glimpsed under the altar of the great basilica of St Paul Outside the Walls. The persecutor and the persecuted, united and martyred for their proclamation of the risen Christ.

The joint testimony of Peter and Paul was rooted in their very different relationships with the risen Jesus. Peter, of course, knew Jesus as a personal friend. Paul had never met Jesus in the flesh, but throughout his writings he testifies to his living sense of the Lord's presence. What both have in common is that their encounters with Jesus occurred within the context of Christian friendship and fellowship, and committed them to active and costly mission in the service of the Gospel. Paul's experience therefore provides a connection between those who knew Jesus personally and all those many Christians who have come to sense his risen presence, and even to see him, during subsequent centuries.

The seer John in the book of Revelation is another crucial link in this chain of living witness. In many ways, Revelation is a sustained reflection upon and celebration of the mystery of the resurrection. Its message is summed up in the words of the risen Jesus to John: "Fear not! I am the First and the Last, the Living One. I was dead but, behold, I am alive for evermore; and I have the keys of death and Hades" (Revelation 1:17–18). For, "Behold, I am making all things new" (Revelation 21:5). The conviction that Christ is present at the heart of the Church and its worship, and supremely in the Eucharist, is expressed in the oldest Christian prayer—*Maranatha*—"Come, Lord!" (1 Corinthians 16:22). In the modern liturgy, this is expressed by the acclamation: "The Lord is here: his Spirit is with us." For great indeed is the mystery of our faith—"Christ has died; Christ is risen; Christ will come again"—because he comes again in our midst now.

So it is that throughout Christian history, and in every part of the Church, Christians have encountered the risen Christ in ways that have changed their lives, and empowered the mission and spiritual life of Christianity. For example, St Bonaventure carefully describes in his *Life of St Francis* how the saint had seven visions of the crucified Christ, the last of which imprinted the stigmata of Christ's sufferings on his body. In the Russian Church, St Seraphim of Sarov, who died in 1834, had a vision of Jesus while serving as a deacon at the altar during the Divine Liturgy. This transfixed him, and the experience became the foundation of his life and sufferings as a hermit and healer.

Recently, an elderly nun told how she too had had such an encounter with Jesus as a young novice while preparing the chapel, which had sustained her vocation for more than fifty years. Priests are often told about such private moments: for example, by an elderly woman, housebound and receiving communion at home, who had once been dying in hospital. "One day, Jesus appeared at the end of my bed, just as he looks in the picture of *The Light of the World*. (This was painted by Holman Hunt and now hangs in St Paul's Cathedral—a popular image often reproduced in the first part of the twentieth century.) He smiled at me, waved his lantern over my bed, and disappeared. It was as simple as that; but the next day I left hospital cured."

The challenge of Eastertide is simply this. If Christ is truly present in our midst, how may we prepare ourselves to encounter him? If he is present among us, are we present with him? For nothing is more frustrating than when a person will not give full attention to someone who is trying to address them! Jesus says to each one of us, "Behold, I stand at the door and knock: if anyone opens the door, I will come in and eat with them and they with me" (Revelation 3:20). There are three simple steps to preparing ourselves to sense his presence and to receive him into the heart of our life. The first is to read a part of a Gospel each day assiduously throughout our life. Only in this way can we accurately perceive the person of Jesus, as it is the genius of the Gospels to convey his character without ever describing him. As we go through life, facets of the Gospel story will engage our understanding and deepen our empathy, as we follow more closely the example of Jesus in our love of God, and in our love for others in his Name.

The second essential step is never to receive Holy Communion unprepared. "This is my Body which is given for you." These solemn words of our Lord command our humble obedience, reverence and love. Sometimes, as we receive Holy Communion, we will sense his presence. Thirdly, as Jesus knocks at the door of each of our hearts, we must make him the centre of our private prayers. Obviously, regular use of the Lord's Prayer, carefully said, builds an immediate bond with his own prayer to his heavenly Father. The Orthodox Jesus Prayer— "Lord Jesus Christ, Son of the Living God, have mercy upon me/us"—addresses Jesus in words drawn from the Gospels, words used by those who met him, and whose lives were changed by him. This prayer can change our lives too, as it has those of so many people across the centuries. It makes a perfect prayer as we read the Gospel each day. It also makes a perfect prayer of preparation for receiving Holy Communion. It can be said quietly anywhere. Let us therefore make these words of the Psalmist our own each day: "When you said to me, 'Seek my Face;' my heart said to you, 'Your Face, O Lord, I will seek'" (Psalm 27:8).

PART 4

Belief and Thought

25

True Priesthood

Hebrews 5:5–10; John 12:20–33

"Sir, we would see Jesus." These words were engraved on a brass plate on the edge of the pulpit in the church where I worshipped with my family to make sure that any preacher kept his eye on the ball. But what shall we see in Jesus as we approach Passiontide? The unknown writer of the letter to the Hebrews has much to say about the costly empathy of Jesus. Perhaps he was a Jewish priest himself, able to reflect on the inner meaning of the ancient and holy rites of his faith, even as he became a Christian. There may also be a hint of criticism of the ways in which priesthood had been corrupted in his own day. For "Christ did not glorify himself", he did not seek to become someone prominent; indeed, as Paul says in his letter to the Philippians, "he emptied himself" (Philippians 2:7). This refusal to claim a position resting upon human approval, tradition or authority is also one of the themes running through the many confrontations that Jesus had with his critics in Jerusalem as recorded in John's Gospel.

The priesthood of Jesus has deeper and more mysterious roots: "You are my son: today I have begotten you." Jesus as the true priest expresses something profound about God himself. "You are a priest forever after the order of Melchizedek"—strange words that allude to the enigmatic figure of a ruling priest whom Abraham encountered during his nomadic existence many centuries earlier (Genesis 14:18–20). His priesthood represents innate human priesthood that antedates the specific priesthood created by Moses and Aaron for the Jewish people. In his offering of bread and wine, Melchizedek became a symbol of the deeper principle of sacrificial priesthood expressed in the Eucharist of

Christianity, as in these words from the Orthodox liturgy, "Thine own, of Thine own, for all and through all we offer Thee, O Lord."

What Jesus revealed was the sacrificial principle that springs from the heart of God himself: for "God so loved the world that he gave his only Son" (John 3:16). Abraham was never closer to the heart of God than when he was willing to offer up his only and beloved son, Isaac. But in that moment, God provided an animal as a substitute, thus ending human sacrifice and intimating something more profound. For only God can offer the sacrifice that makes peace between himself and sinful human beings; and this sacrifice was made once and for all by the death of Jesus on the Cross. In the words of the *Book of Common Prayer*, "He made there by his one oblation of himself once offered, a full, perfect and sufficient sacrifice, oblation and satisfaction for the sins of the whole world."

The sacrifice that found its fullest expression on Calvary was evident also in the ministry of Jesus, especially in his prayer and in his compassion. The writer of the letter to the Hebrews knew stories about Jesus to which he alluded when he wrote about his profound empathy that was deepened by his painful and sacrificial prayer. The ethos of the ministry of Jesus was summed up in his prayer, "Thy will be done." The writer perhaps remembered in particular the agony of Jesus in the Garden of Gethsemane, "who in the days of his flesh, offered up prayers and supplications with strong crying and tears to him that was able to save him from death". His ultimate and willing obedience expressed perfectly his relation as Son to his Father. His human suffering was the crucible of divine perfecting through which divine remaking flows out into the life of humanity. This is part of the meaning of the healing miracles of Jesus. How can we envisage this divine remaking? Just as healthy cells in the human body have to combat alien viruses and infections, so healthy individual human "cells", in which the love of God dwells by his Holy Spirit, can transform gradually the whole corporate existence of humanity. This is part of the meaning of being the Body of Christ, and it is the great hope for all human beings, as Christ becomes indwelling in our lives. In the words of Paul, "God made Christ, who knew no sin, to be sin on our behalf, so that we might become the righteousness of God in him" (2 Corinthians 5:21). His suffering for sin is the antidote to our corruption: his life becomes eternal life like water springing up within us (John 4:14).

The hallmark of divine indwelling is always a deeper empathy, the capacity to reach out in prayer and compassion to those around us, and to respond sensitively to their needs: "If someone wants to serve me, let that person follow me" (Mark 8:34). How? By accepting the principle of living through dying. Someone who loves their own life selfishly will lose it in the end; but someone who is prepared to repudiate this impulse will keep it forever by self-giving love. God will recognize such a person as his own child, a true brother or sister to Jesus himself. Just as seed has to be planted in the ground in order to generate fruitful life, so a person has to be buried in the ground of humility by Christ-like compassion and heartfelt prayer. The desire to serve others after the example of Jesus must be rooted in diligent prayer, as both have their source in the desire for God himself, who is Love.

The Cross of Christ was the culmination of his compassion and mission that overturned the corrupt values of human society, casting out the selfish and cruel principles of evil itself. Only God can rescue humanity in this way, and he did so by becoming a human person in Jesus, who said: "If I am lifted up from the earth, I will draw everyone to myself" (John 12:32). The phrase "lifted up" intimated the manner of his death—by crucifixion; and it provoked immediate controversy: for how could the Messiah as God's Chosen One become God's Cursed One? The phrase may also hint at resurrection, by being "lifted out of the earth" itself, from the humiliation of burial to the glory of heaven. It is only through the Cross, however, that the light of God shines in this searching way into each human heart, posing a fateful choice to every human being, here and hereafter.

Sacrifice, compassion, empathy and obedience: by each of these the downward steps of Adam and Eve are reversed; and the Gospels record how this was evident in the life of Jesus. These become the hallmarks of Christian saints, who have been made like him. This weekend, our church recalls St Cuthbert, one of the earliest and best loved of the Anglo-Saxon saints, representing the first generation of home-grown Christian leadership and ministry in England in the seventh century. He was born around the year 634, the beneficiary of the mission of St

Aidan of Lindisfarne, who arrived there around that time. Cuthbert became a monk at Melrose and was the prior there around the year 660. From there, he moved to lead the monastic community on Lindisfarne itself that had been founded by Aidan; but in 676 he retired to become a hermit on the Inner Farne island close by. In 685, Cuthbert was pressed by the king of Northumbria and others to become a bishop based at Lindisfarne. He threw himself into pastoral ministry and evangelism, visiting remote villages of both Anglo-Saxons and Britons. He became known for his prophetic teaching and his capacity to heal the sick. He died on 20 March 687 on the Inner Farne, where a chapel still stands that commemorates him.

The first anonymous *Life of Cuthbert* was later enhanced and rewritten in prose and poetry by Bede himself; and the famous Lindisfarne Gospels were inspired by the cult that grew up at his shrine in the monastery of Lindisfarne. Many years later, his relics were transferred to Durham, where they now lie in the cathedral, accompanied by treasures found in his coffin, which date from his time and later. For many centuries his body remained incorrupt as a sign of his sanctity. One of the distinctive features of Bede's *Life of Cuthbert* is the vivid first-hand account that he included of how Cuthbert died on the Inner Farne, cut off from his friends for many days by raging storms and lying seriously ill. This fierce spiritual conflict with his ancient foe marked him out as a truly Christ-like person. He said to his friend who finally made it across to the island, "My adversaries have never persecuted me so frequently during all the time that I have lived on this island as during these last five days." Cuthbert thus entered Passiontide, and through his own suffering, in life and in death, divine life flowed for the healing of many people.

26

Breaking Barriers

Ephesians 2:11–22

No one can follow the news or read history without being acutely aware of the appalling problem that afflicts human societies everywhere. From remote archaeological sites, throughout ancient history and the Middle Ages, and into the modern period, the capacity of human beings for mutual destruction is chronic and disastrous. In the last century, millions died as a result. One reason why a crudely evolutionary view of the human species is so defective is its inability to account for the wanton, deliberate and cruel ways in which human beings often act so ruthlessly against their interests as a species. The creation of nuclear weapons epitomizes this. In our own time, this negative impact on other human beings can be seen as closely connected to our negative impact upon the environment that sustains our common life.

In the language of the Bible, this is the meaning of sin—the consequences of repudiating any sense of accountability towards God, whose world it is, or belief in him, whose children we all are. The rebellion and curse of Cain stalks every human generation, expressed in the mocking words: "Am I my brother's keeper?" (Genesis 4:9). The Bible itself is a stark record of human wrongdoing: it is also a record of God's challenge to human beings who behave in this way. This is why the Bible is often banned in dictatorships as too threatening a book to be read openly or even privately.

At the heart of human history stands the Cross of Christ: God's ultimate challenge to, and also his remedy for, human sinfulness. In the letter to the Ephesians, as elsewhere, Paul addressed the great divide within his own society between Jews and Gentiles. His whole mission was one of active and costly repentance as a devout Jew to enable non-Jews to enter into the inheritance of God's people through faith in Jesus Christ. He spoke directly to the sense of hopelessness and alienation that many people experienced, then as now, the sense of being cut off from God or of being second-rate as human beings. One of the most malign expressions of sinfulness is when people define their own identity, religious, racial or political, at the expense of others, turning them into scapegoats and targets of prejudice and discrimination. The end of this process is genocide.

The death of Christ on the Cross shatters forever this ghastly barrier of mutual separation between human beings. Only the shed blood of Christ can bring about the inner change and healing within human nature that can liberate people from this tendency to persecute and crucify others. In the words of the *Book of Common Prayer*: "He made there by his one oblation of himself once offered, a full, perfect and sufficient sacrifice, oblation, and satisfaction for the sins of the whole world." In Christianity, the weekly celebration of the Eucharist demonstrates the basic truth that all Christians are now one humanity in Jesus Christ. At the altar rail there can be no discrimination on grounds of race or ethnicity, of class or education. One cup and one bread are offered by all, to all, and for all: "Thine own, of thine own, for all and through all we offer thee, O Lord." This is why as Anglicans we welcome to Holy Communion all who would normally receive communion in their own church. It is the Lord's Supper of reconciliation and renewal, and it is not the property of any particular church.

The Cross of Christ plunges like a scalpel into the deep place of the human heart where enmity and hostility lurk. We are not truly becoming Christians if our inner attitudes are not being continually challenged and changed by encountering Christ in the pages of the Gospels, receiving him in the sacrament, and seeing him in the faces and needs of others. As Jesus said, "Inasmuch as you care for the least of these my brethren you are caring for me" (Matthew 25:40). His parable of the Good Samaritan and his own actions stand forever as stern rebukes to the mocking words, "Am I my brother's keeper?"

Paul teaches that human reconciliation only occurs when it springs from being reconciled to God himself. In the Garden of Eden, the root of original sin stands revealed as disobedience towards God, and contempt towards him and all that he has made. Christ came into human history to reverse the downward path of sinful humanity. He came to destroy the sense of hostility that has poisoned human attitudes towards God and towards each other. Christ's purpose was to reconcile all human beings to God, and so to each other, "in one body unto God through the Cross".

The coming of Christ also addresses the deep unease and restlessness that stirs in the depths of human life, and which expresses itself in so many empty values and frustrated desires; for as St Augustine said, "Our hearts are restless until they find their rest in God." There can be no inner peace that is not rooted in peace with God. But peace with God means being obedient once again to his love; and herein lies the problem: the unruly wills and affections of sinful human beings. In Christ, God comes to everyone who will listen to him with the loving challenge: "Do you know what you really want—whom do you seek?"

Paul's vision was a very positive one, evident elsewhere in his writings, as in other parts of the New Testament. It is of a new humanity, restored in its relationship to God and able once again to experience and to express the love of God to others and towards the created world. This message of hope is of urgent significance today. "Through Christ we all have access in one Spirit to the Father." In these words, the mystery at the heart of Christianity is intimated—how human beings are being drawn within the love of God the Trinity, Father, Son and Holy Spirit.

The reality of the Church stands as God's sign in human existence of the possibility of reconciliation with him and a new creation. Its existence in history is found in the lives of its saints in every age—"the household of God". Christianity, with its rich history, gives to human beings a new and deep sense of identity, belonging and unity; and that sense of inner security enables people to welcome others openly and lovingly as fellow children of God. Christian ethics and Christian worship stand or fall together, as the Christian community becomes, under the guidance of the Holy Spirit, a sacred and loving environment, "a holy temple to the Lord". Elsewhere, Paul indicated that this reality is rooted in each human person, made in the divine image, who in their bodies become sanctuaries of the Holy Spirit. The transformation of each person is thus the key to the transformation of the whole Body of Christ.

27

Faith Seeking Understanding

A sermon for the feast of St Thomas the Apostle

John 20:24–31

The testimony of Thomas lies at the heart of the apostolic foundation of the Church. His soubriquet "doubting" is completely misleading, as the evangelist clearly placed this story carefully at the conclusion of his Gospel. The prologue of the Gospel ends with the assertion that "no-one has seen God at any time: God the Only-begotten, the Son in the bosom of the Father, he has expressed him" (John 1:18). The declaration of Thomas that Jesus is "my Lord and my God!" reveals how someone may come to a living faith, and truly perceive that "Jesus is the Christ, the Son of God, and by believing you may have life in his name".

What is the nature of Christian faith? This story shows that such faith is not blind faith, which has no place in Christianity; for true faith does not suppress questioning: it is likely to prompt it. Thomas was clearly alert to the dangers of mass hallucination, self-deception, wishful thinking, and fantasy born of bitter bereavement and disappointed hopes. His reticence sprang from his loyalty to Jesus, his love for a lost friend. The resurrection of someone who had died such a terrible death was clearly inconceivable and improbable, whatever his friends might say. He articulated what anyone considering the Gospel testimony might reasonably feel. How can this thing be?

The timing of this story is also significant because in the New Testament and early Christianity the eighth day signified the new age of God's kingdom, the first day of a new creation. In some ways, this appearance of Jesus has similarities to the Transfiguration, as his resurrection ushers in the promised new age. Jesus invited Thomas to reach out and to touch him—through the livid scars of his wounds. His resurrection was real because it was actual, as were his sufferings, even if his bodily presence was no longer confined to time and space. His voice, his touch, his face, his wounds—all were recognizable, and loveable too. In a moment, their relationship was affirmed and transformed. Christian faith is therefore about personal trust in Jesus, as God reaches out through him to human beings, saying to them personally, "Adam, where are you?" (Genesis 3:9).

In the Middle Ages, theologians like Augustine, Anselm and Bonaventure set great store by the principle of "faith seeking understanding"—*fides quaerens intellectum*. This has its root in an early Latin translation of a text in Isaiah, "Unless you believe you will not understand" (Isaiah 7:9). In fact, the Hebrew meaning is, "Unless you believe you will not be established." This further deepens the meaning of the text, for "to understand" is to stand in the right place before God, under the Cross of Christ, the only place of ultimate truth for human beings. The goal of Christian faith is true understanding. How then does faith seek understanding, and what might this understanding mean?

In any relationship, there has to be intelligent and loving trust, as no-one can ever fully understand another person. Such trust enables someone to apprehend truly what they can never fully comprehend— another person; and this is as true of human beings as it is also true of God. A marriage is a demonstration of this kind of intelligent, loving and purposeful trust, always seeking a fuller understanding of another person, but never possessing them. Such trust is also crucial in the nurture and upbringing of children. As we approach Christ in our prayers, we can make our own the prayer in the Gospel: "Lord, I believe: help my unbelief!" (Mark 9:24). In biblical and medieval thought, "to know" means to enter into, and to participate in what is known. Thus "to observe" is not the same as "to know". Modern thought, however, tends to make "understanding" rest upon complete detachment and objectivity. Christian understanding, however, is rooted in intuition as well as in reason, both united in love.

The word "seeking" implies a continuing process of discovery, just as in a marriage or in a strong friendship, or in the development of a child. Seeking implies an orientation of the heart and of the will, which in turn guide and inform the mind. What, or whom, do you most truly seek? As Christians we are called to seek God with our whole heart, and to heed the call of Christ to follow him. Thomas was seeking the truth about Jesus, and through his human relationship with him, now restored and transformed, he was able to sense and perceive his divine nature. But this was only mediated to him through the marks of the crucifixion, by what St Paul describes as "the wisdom of the Cross" (1 Corinthians 1:17f). Thus, "I will seek him whom my soul loves, and when I found him, I would not let him go" (Song of Songs 3:2–4). The questioning of Thomas expressed his heartfelt grief and love; it manifested his inner seeking of Jesus. His acclamation expressed his joy at finding, beyond all hope, his beloved friend again.

What then is the nature of "understanding" in Christianity? It is interesting that in English, the word is very basic and not primarily intellectual. It means "to stand under" and in the right place, and not necessarily fully to comprehend. Perhaps the words of the Psalmist capture its true spirit in relation to God: "When I consider Thy heavens, the work of Thy fingers, the moon and the stars which Thou has ordained; what is man that Thou art mindful of him? Or the son of man that Thou visitest him?" (Psalm 8:1–4). He, or she, was standing under the great canopy of the stars, not polluted by other light, overawed by the magnificence and wonder of creation. This sense of wonder and respectful awe lies at the heart of Christian understanding—seeing the world for what it is, the beautiful expression and reflection of divine glory.

It was in this spirit that Thomas exclaimed to Jesus, who was standing before him, "My Lord and my God." He saw him in a new and true light, the light of the resurrection, and was blessed in so doing (cf. Psalm 36:9). This beatific vision, however, was intimated to him only through the suffering humanity of his friend, who was also his Lord. His honesty and response, and his vision, were affirmed in the last known beatitude of Jesus: "Blessed are they that have not seen but yet have believed." The testimony of Thomas is therefore the final sign in this Gospel that enables subsequent generations of Christians to have confidence in the witness of the apostles to the resurrection of Jesus as "Christ and the Son of God", whom they knew and loved as their friend. Thomas spoke for them all; and by embracing the wounded hands of Jesus, he points the way for all those who would seek to love and know the risen Christ in spirit and in truth.

These words of St Paul make a fine commentary on the meaning and significance of this encounter: "I beseech you therefore by the mercies of God to present your bodies as a living sacrifice, holy and well-pleasing to God, which is your spiritual worship. Do not be conformed to this world, but be transformed by the renewal of your mind, so that you may prove for yourself what is the good and acceptable and perfect will of God" (Romans 12:1–2). For in his will is our peace.

2 8

The Transfiguration

Mark 9:2–9

In many ways, the account of the Transfiguration of Jesus is the centrepoint of Mark's Gospel. The opening message of Jesus that "the time is fulfilled and the kingdom of God is at hand: repent and believe the gospel" (Mark 1:15) posed the key question in the first part of this Gospel: is Jesus truly the Messiah? It is notable that initially it was only demonic forces of evil that actually recognized who he was: "I know who you are—the Holy One of God" (Mark 1:24). To human beings around him, however, including his closest disciples, such recognition came much more slowly, as they recalled vividly and long after the event, when this Gospel was being written down. Their uncertainty revolved around the mysterious use of the title "Son of Man" by Jesus to intimate who he was and wherein lay his authority to heal and to forgive sins (Mark 2:10). "The Son of Man is Lord even of the Sabbath" (Mark 2:28), and to the consternation of his critics, Jesus demonstrated this by healing in synagogues on the Sabbath day. When Jesus was exorcising people, to his embarrassment, demons often cried out, "You are the Son of God!" (Mark 3:11).

Following Jesus was challenging to say the least for his disciples. Pitching dangerously in a storm on the Sea of Galilee, Jesus arose unperturbed from sleep to still the storm—in nature as well as in their own hearts. "Who is this that even the wind and the sea obey him?" (Mark 4:41). In a later storm, he hailed them from the surface of the sea with the awesome words, "Cheer up! I AM. Do not be afraid" (Mark 6:50). They then witnessed the deliverance of a deranged foreigner raging among tombs in his distress. The unhappy man fled to Jesus and the evil within him acclaimed him openly as "Son of the Most High God" (Mark

5:7). When Jesus raised the daughter of Jairus, their minds went back to the miracles of Elijah and Elisha, by which the coming of the Messiah would be measured: for raising the dead was a pre-eminent sign of his presence, and there are three accounts of Jesus doing this on separate occasions in the Gospels. The Feeding of the Five Thousand was another decisive moment of recognition, so it is recorded in all four Gospels. In this Gospel, there is also a second feeding miracle of comparable scale; and for Jesus "bread broken" was a catalyst for their recognition of who he was (Mark 8:17-21).

The story of the Transfiguration is preceded in Mark by two very significant miracles: the healing of a deaf and dumb man, which led people to acclaim Jesus in words anticipating the coming of the Messiah in the Old Testament prophets (Mark 7:37), and most strikingly that of a blind person, who had to have his sight healed in a double sense so that he could rightly interpret what he saw (Mark 8:23-5). It is in this precise context that Peter's decisive recognition of Jesus as the Christ—the Messiah—occurs. It was only by gradual steps that those closest to him came to sense and see who he truly was. In response, Jesus promised them a glimpse of the coming kingdom of God (Mark 9:1). Mark's Gospel is therefore a Gospel of epiphany, describing how the hidden light of Jesus increasingly seeped through his actions and his person.

The Transfiguration itself was an intensely private moment, witnessed only by three disciples who were closest to Jesus—Peter, James and John. They alone had witnessed the raising of the daughter of Jairus in the presence of her parents (Mark 5:37); and they were to witness the agony of Jesus in the Garden of Gethsemane (Mark 14:33). In Jewish law, three witnesses sufficed. They each appear in Orthodox icons in representative poses—astonished, overwhelmed, and rapt in contemplation. Indeed, an icon gives the best way to think about the Gospel story of the Transfiguration, because the evangelist has painted a potent word-picture, whose imagery is drawn from the Old Testament. The high mountain recalls Sinai where the glory of the Lord descended and was witnessed at first hand by Moses and more distantly by the people of Israel. The Greek word used for transfiguration in the Gospel is *metamorphosis*. The light of God shines through the human person of Jesus, who was transformed and not consumed by it, rather like the

Burning Bush in Exodus 3. As Paul said in 2 Corinthians, "God who commanded light to shine out of darkness has shone in our hearts to give the illumination of the knowledge of the glory of God in the face of Jesus Christ" (2 Corinthians 4:6). Or in the words of the prologue of John's Gospel, "we saw his glory, the glory of the only-begotten from the Father" (John 1:14; cf. 1 John 1:1–5).

Jesus appeared in dialogue with Moses and Elijah, both of whom had encountered God long before on Sinai. It is as if the precious shell that had long contained the mystery of the Word of God, and to which they had testified, now broke open, and the living person stepped out to fulfil what had been promised. The response of Peter was significant as Jews believe that when the Messiah comes, they will gather with him on the mountain of the Lord and safely resume their essentially nomadic existence: they commemorate this hope each year at the Feast of Tabernacles. Peter expressed the expectation of his contemporaries; and the prologue of John's Gospel declares that the Word of God "pitched his tent" among us (John 1:14). "It is good for us to be here!" In these words of Peter is expressed the sense that they were in the promised presence of God himself: the word "good" in Greek—*kalos*—means wonderful, beautiful, stupendous, and it is used in Genesis 1 to describe the Creation itself. Beauty precedes life itself because it reflects and expresses the glory of God now seen focused in the face of Jesus Christ.

The three disciples were overwhelmed by the sense of God's presence in Jesus, and it is notable that in Hebrew the word for "divine glory"—*kabod*—means something heavy and imposing, inducing "the fear of the Lord". The cloud recalled again the story of Sinai, the experience of both Moses and Elijah, the brooding sense of the invisible God. As before on Sinai, the moment of epiphany was a supreme moment of divine self-expression: for as at the Baptism of Jesus, another private moment, now the voice of God acclaimed Jesus as "my Beloved Son—listen to him". When they looked up, they saw only Jesus. John's prologue concludes with the declaration that while "no-one has seen God at any time, God the only-begotten, the Son in the heart of the Father, he has expressed him" (John 1:18). This is the reason why Christians worship Jesus as divine, as the Son of God and the fullest expression of his Being, as, in the words of the Creed, "God from God and Light from Light." For in

Jesus the image and likeness of God is fully revealed, and humanity finds its true measure and vocation. In words paraphrasing St Irenaeus, "The vision of God is the life of humanity and the glory of God is the living human person."

The mystery of this moment remained hidden for some time, though it is alluded to elsewhere, notably in 2 Peter (1:16–21) and probably in Hebrews too (1:1–3; cf. Colossians 1:15–19; 2:9). The three disciples were commanded to keep their experience secret until after the resurrection, to which it pointed. For there is an intimate connection between the mountain of Transfiguration and the hill of Calvary, as Luke makes clear in his account of this event: Moses and Elijah were discussing with Jesus the destiny—*exodos*—that he was to accomplish in Jerusalem, the destruction of evil and the deliverance of humanity by his own death on the Cross (Luke 9:31). This Gospel tells the same message, because Peter's moment of recognition which heralded the Transfiguration of Jesus prompted the first explicit prediction by Jesus of his Passion, revealing the meaning of his mysterious title "Son of Man" (Mark 8:31). The rest of Mark's Gospel is then determined by this urgent question: if Jesus is truly the Messiah, why must the Son of Man suffer and die? It is this question that leads us also into the season of Lent each year.

29

The Name of the Lord

A sermon for the feast of the Holy Name of Jesus

It is a matter of great regret that this feast of the Holy Name of Jesus is no longer included in the Roman or Anglican calendars. Alongside the Transfiguration, which immediately precedes it, this feast on 7 August survived in the calendar of the *Book of Common Prayer*. It was popularized in the Western church by the Franciscans at the end of the Middle Ages, and its observance has left an indelible impression on Christian prayer and devotion.

The story of the Burning Bush in Exodus 3 is the root of Jewish and later Christian veneration of the Holy Name of the Lord; veneration of the Names of Allah is also found in Islam. Moses encountered God and received the Name of God as I AM WHO I AM (Exodus 3:14). In later Judaism, the Name of God was regarded as so holy that it was not pronounced explicitly when reading Scripture, or in prayers. In the ancient world, the giving of a personal name was a rare privilege that gave someone access to that person. It was guarded as closely as a modern PIN number. In revealing his Name and something of his nature to Moses, God gave something of himself in a way which human beings could receive and respond to in a relationship with him.

The promise of the vision of God is apparent throughout the Old Testament as a great hope. It is striking, however, that the promise of a vision of God was first given in order to bring about the rescue of God's people from slavery and genocide in Egypt. In the Old Testament, the hope of deliverance sprang from prophetic vision, and in Judaism at the time of Jesus, the holy Name of the Lord was solemnly celebrated in the Temple in Jerusalem. This is part of the background to the prominent emphasis placed by the earliest Christians on the Name of Jesus as the key to human salvation: "for there is no other Name given among human beings by which we must be saved" (Acts 4:12).

In the New Testament, the Name of Jesus brought healing and deliverance. It also lay at the heart of early Christian worship, as expressed in the Aramaic prayer *Maranatha!*—"Our Lord comes", or "O Lord, come!" (1 Corinthians 16:22). In his letter to the Philippians, Paul included an early hymn to the holy Name of Jesus: "God highly exalted him, and gave him the Name which is above every name; so that at the Name of Jesus every knee should bow ... and every tongue confess that Jesus Christ is Lord, to the glory of God the Father" (Philippians 2:9–11).

Devotion to the Name of Jesus is apparent in both Eastern and Western churches. The practice of the Jesus Prayer was established by the fifth century among monastic communities, as habitual prayer that later came to be linked to breathing as a form of profound meditation: "Lord Jesus Christ, Son of the living God: have mercy upon me, a sinner." In Anglo-Saxon England, devotion to the person of Jesus was intense and direct, and by the twelfth century, under the leadership of St Bernard of Clairvaux and the Cistercians, this took the form of meditation on, and delight in, the Name of Jesus, bringing his presence close to the heart. The beautiful hymn *Jesu Dulcis Memoria* dates from this time, and it underlies many lovely translations in modern hymnbooks. Subsequent Franciscan evangelism developed a cult of the Holy Name of Jesus that left its mark on the piety of the Reformation and Counter-Reformation. In English Christianity, the eighteenth century witnessed some remarkable hymns composed by Wesley and others in devotion to the Name of Jesus, which are well-loved today. It is a pity that the feast of the Holy Name is not commemorated as a fine ecumenical celebration of so rich a spiritual tradition evident in all churches.

How should we reverence the Holy Name of Jesus today? The Jesus Prayer gives us a sure guide. This prayer is not simply a meditative mantra; nor should devotion to the Name of Jesus result in some kind of cult of his person that becomes idealized, subjective or remote. It is first and foremost a prayer of worship and deep devotion, a conscious and humble coming into the presence of the Lord in response to him as he comes to us, knocking on the door of our hearts (Revelation 3:20).

Prayer at home in the presence of the Lord in this way prepares us for sensing his presence in the mystery of the Eucharist in church. It makes an excellent preparation for receiving Holy Communion.

We have also to make sure that we are actually addressing Jesus as he is portrayed in the four Gospels. Their genius is to convey a real sense of his person and character, without at any time trying to define or describe him. Devotion to the Holy Name of Jesus should always be anchored in regular reading of the Gospels and meditation upon them. Only by reflecting carefully and prayerfully on the picture they give of Jesus in action, his teaching and his attitude to others, can we be sure that we are actually following him, as he has called us to do. The Jesus Prayer is excellent preparation for reading the Gospels.

The Jesus Prayer is a great expression of the love and devotion that should be personal and central in our lives as Christians. This love is echoed in the lovely hymns in the Western church that speak of the Name and Person of Jesus: "Jesus, the very thought of thee" or "Jesu, thou joy of loving hearts". These are derived from the Latin hymn *Jesus Dulcis Memoria*. No less moving is a hymn from the eighteenth century, "How sweet the name of Jesus sounds in a believer's ear". There are many modern hymns that pick up this theme, notably "Shine, Jesus, shine". Jesus calls us to love him as our Saviour and also as our friend; but this can only come about if he is truly the Lord of our lives.

Life in Christ never proceeds as a straight line of development, however, but rather as a spiral of dynamic spiritual development, circling around Christ and his Cross. This is a movement marked by purification, illumination and perfection, in the sense that the Spirit of Christ is always purifying, illuminating and perfecting our lives as they unfold. The Jesus Prayer contains this pattern implicitly. It is firstly an act of adoration—"Lord Jesus Christ"—and also of penitence—"have mercy upon me, a sinner." This is always the truth about our relationship with Christ, just as it was true for those in the Gospels who first encountered him. It is secondly a prayer of, and for, illumination as we also pray to the Holy Spirit, "Enable with perpetual light the dullness of our blinded sight." Only then can we begin to see what it means to acclaim Jesus as "the Son of the Living God", transfigured, crucified, risen and glorified.

It is finally a prayer of perfecting as we permit the Spirit of Christ to move in the depths of our hearts, to cleanse, reform and transform our lives, and to make us more truly Christ-like, as God's children being restored in the image and likeness of God himself. This is why we close every prayer "through Jesus Christ our Lord", confident that he alone is the one who can bring security and healing to our lives, as he embraces us within his boundless love. He seeks our hearts, and devotion to his Holy Name is a profound way of giving our hearts to him throughout our lives.

3 0

The Spirit Within

John 15:16–27

I remember my father often saying to me as a young person that the Church needs to give much fuller attention to the reality and person of the Holy Spirit. At that time, the Charismatic Movement was attracting attention and concern in equal measure. Whether it has prompted a deeper understanding of the Holy Spirit is an open question. The difficulty for many Christians remains that, whereas they have some real sense of who Jesus was, and is, from the Gospels, it is often very hard to envisage the Holy Spirit.

The roots of Christian belief in the Holy Spirit lie deep in the Old Testament. There are two Hebrew words used for "spirit". One word—*ruach*—is used to describe the rushing hot wind of the desert that sweeps all before it, such as a person might experience getting off a plane in a very hot country. The other word—*nephesh*—speaks of the subtle breath of the Holy Spirit as the life-giver and creator; for no breath, no life.

What is distinctive about the teaching of Jesus in the Fourth Gospel is his insistence on the personal nature of the Holy Spirit: "When he, the Advocate (or Comforter) comes, whom I will send to you from the Father, who is the Spirit of Truth and who comes from the Father, ... he will guide you into all truth" (John 16:13). It is this quiet insistence on the personal nature of the Holy Spirit that begins to reveal to us the mystery of the Holy Trinity, as the communion of the Father, the Son and the Holy Spirit into which we are being drawn by divine love.

How does the Bible enable us to sense the reality of the Holy Spirit? Paul speaks about the gifts of the Spirit, so evident in the rich diversity of human responses to God within the historical and modern life of the worldwide Church. Note that Paul speaks of gifts in a way that challenges any religion based on merit or achievement, for you cannot possess what God may give you. Some may be able to teach, others to preach; some will have vocations of healing and listening; others are more practical in their Christian life and service. What is important is not the equality of endowment or activity, but rather the equality of value of each unique person in whom the Holy Spirit dwells. The Holy Spirit enables the varied natural gifts of human beings to be transformed and to shine forth in a life-giving way, as each human person in their individual uniqueness mirrors something true and loving about the uniqueness of God; for all are one in Jesus Christ.

Paul also speaks about the fruits of the Spirit in a way that echoes the parables and teaching of Jesus himself. Fruit takes time to mature and grow, it cannot be hurried. Fruit springs from the inner life of a plant, its nurture, health and development. Without the inner water of life provided by the Holy Spirit, no Christian can bear fruit that will last. Fruit is not an achievement, however: it is a sign of grace, given for the wellbeing of others and according to divine purpose. It is also the result of accepting sometimes painful pruning. Love, joy, peace, patience, kindness, goodness, gentleness and so forth set a searching standard by which we must measure and reform our lives. This standard of Christ-like love should also govern how we relate to other people; for you cannot act love: you have to be it. Indeed, a priest who is not a pastor is a poseur. We can easily prevent the life of the Holy Spirit within us, but we cannot contrive it or hurry it, let alone possess it. Fruit, like life itself, is a gift of God to us and through us; and it is by the fruits of our life that our faith is found to be true or not.

This is because human beings are designed to become "sanctuaries of the Holy Spirit" (1 Corinthians 6:19). Our personalities are designed to become windows through which the invisible light and love of the Spirit can shine. The altar of the heart is the deep inner place where we may sense the hidden presence of the Holy Spirit within us if we truly seek him there. We have to mean what we say when we pray, "Come, Holy Spirit, fill now the hearts of your faithful people: and kindle within us the fire of your love."

It is very interesting that the sense of the Holy Spirit is conveyed to us in the Bible by various natural metaphors and symbols. For example, fire which is warming and encouraging, but at the same time challenging, purifying and burning in its impact. Or water, without which there can be no life at all, but which can also destroy by sweeping away whatever is false in our lives. Or light, by which we may begin to see things in the light of God's love for us and for others, but which may at times almost blind us by stretching our vision, before "enabling the dullness of our blinded sight". Or oil, a symbol of gentleness and healing that also exposes in a stinging way our inner sin and disease. When we pray, "Lord, have mercy"—*Kyrie Eleison*—the word *eleison* signifies being anointed with the healing oil of God's love, "to whom all hearts are open, all desires known and from whom no secrets are hidden".

Supremely, the Holy Spirit comes among us in the sacraments of Baptism and Holy Communion. Christians are only born again, and from above, by water and the Spirit. The bread and wine of Holy Communion are consecrated by the words of Jesus and by invoking the descent of the Holy Spirit. Like the prophet Isaiah in the Temple, we have to receive the Spirit's presence in communion as a burning coal taken from the heavenly altar of God to purge our lips and our hearts. It is in the chalice upon the altar that we see that which we are called to become: someone who is open, stable, clean, and ready to receive the fire of the Spirit within the heart of our life.

In all these ways, the reality of the Holy Spirit may be sought and sensed; but how may he be envisaged? The fact that elements within the created world are potent sacramental symbols of his reality and presence is surely highly significant. The Bible interprets to us afresh how the whole created world is resplendent with the glory of the living God who created it. The Spirit's presence may also be sensed and seen in the lives and personalities of saints, who are people in whom his presence has transformed their characters in their own lifetime and for eternity. A saint has been defined as someone who makes God real, who is truly Christ-like, and from whom the fire of the Spirit's love springs forth to kindle love in the hearts of others, often in a healing way. For in their lives the Holy Spirit has come to dwell.

Here is the testimony of a British saint, Patrick, in his *Confession* to the reality of the Holy Spirit in his life. He learnt to pray the hard way as a captured slave on the west coast of Ireland, from where he escaped, and to where he returned as a missionary in the fifth century:

> One night, either within me or beside me, someone was speaking in a most elegant language, which I listened to but could not understand, except that at the end of it he said to me, "he who gave his life for you, he it is who is speaking within you." I woke up full of joy.
>
> Another time I saw him praying within me, almost above my body and my inner self: he was praying earnestly with deep groans. While this was happening, I was wondering who it could be praying like this within me; but at the end of his prayer, he told me that he was the Holy Spirit. I woke up and then I remembered the words of the apostle Paul (in Romans 8:26).

Just as a glittering crystal chandelier may refract and reflect in manifold splendour the single light that is within it, so the lives of the saints refract and reflect the manifold grace of the Holy Spirit, giving him expression through each unique personality that has been made in the divine image and restored in the divine likeness, in very specific historical situations. Very often it is through a saint, known or unknown, that the Holy Spirit draws nigh to communicate with us and to change our lives: for his self-effacing humility is that of Christ himself.

3 1

The Communion of the Trinity

In the Nicene Creed, we profess belief in one God, a belief that we share with Jews, from whom Christianity derives, and also with Islam, which inherited this belief from Jews and Christians. Christianity, however, is distinctive as a monotheistic faith in what it believes about the nature of the oneness of God.

Christian belief in the three persons of the Trinity, the Father, the Son and the Holy Spirit, springs from the explicit teaching and language of Jesus himself, as recorded in the Gospels and expressed in the rest of the New Testament. Jesus called God his Father using the word *Abba* that a child would use for its parent: "Our Father who art in heaven." It is notable that, in the early writing of St Paul, this word had already passed into Christian prayer: "God sent forth the Spirit of his Son into our hearts, crying *Abba*, Father" (Galatians 4:6; cf. Romans 8:15–16). Indeed, this text epitomizes and expresses early Christian belief in the three persons of God.

In the Old Testament, belief in the Holy Spirit is evident in the story of creation, the anointing of prophets and kings, and in the outpouring of divine wisdom that is celebrated and expressed in the wisdom literature of the Bible. What is distinctive in the New Testament, however, is the way in which the Holy Spirit is perceived to be a distinct person, given by God through Christ; in the words of Jesus: "When he the Spirit of Truth comes, he will guide you into all truth" (John 16:13).

Belief in the Trinitarian nature of God is only revealed in and through the person of Jesus Christ as God's Son. He came into the world to restore human beings as God's children. He revealed the depth of his relationship with his Father, even to agony and death on the Cross. The earliest witnesses perceived how the outpouring of the Holy Spirit flowed through his death on the Cross. The coming of the Holy Spirit confirmed forever the significance of each human being, created in the image and likeness of God, and designed to become the sanctuary of the indwelling Spirit of God.

Belief in the Trinity is therefore not a logical construct of the human mind, nor are terms like "Father" or "Son" simply human analogies projected onto God. They are terms of personal address, hallowed by Christ himself, and as his words they transcend their normal gender-defined usage. To be a Christian is to be drawn into the communion of love that is the heart of God. As Jesus said: "If a person loves me, he will keep my word: and my Father will love him; and *we* will come to him, and make our dwelling with him" (John 14:23).

Christians believe that God's being is his goodness, which overflows in creative and redeeming love, for "God is love". It is the nature of love to be self-giving, to seek to love another person, and to unite with that person in a common and creative love. The Father loves the Son, and endows him with the fullness of his own power of love: from their united love springs the Holy Spirit, who completes the communion of divine love. Some sense of the profound reality of this mystery of divine love may be experienced within the sacrament of Christian marriage, inasmuch as a man marrying a woman gives himself fully to her and she to him, freely and willingly, in a covenant of mutual love. In due time, and by the grace of God, they unite in their love to share with God in the creation of another human person, who is loved equally by them both, and also by God himself. This is why Christian marriage and the loving nurture of children is at the heart of Christianity and the life of the Church.

PART 5

Communion of Love

3 2

Christian Marriage

A sermon for a wedding

"In the Name of the Father, and of the Son, and of the Holy Spirit. Amen." These words are too easily said, but something of their full force strikes home when we meet to consecrate a Christian marriage. Promises are taken in the presence of God, and rings are blessed in the name of the Holy Trinity, as is the marriage itself. These actions have a deep solemnity in terms of the human and personal commitment that is being made. They also signify that a marriage is being placed willingly and lovingly into the hands of God; or, more precisely, it is to be enfolded in the love that flows within God as three persons, Father, Son and Holy Spirit, for "God is love". How can this be, and what might it mean?

When we think of God the Father, we take our cue from the prayer and teaching of Jesus himself. What he demonstrated by word and deed was his complete trust in God as his loving Father, someone whom he could address as *Abba*—the word a child would use to its father. He invites us each day to address God in the same way as "Our Father". This trust was, of course, put to a bitter test at the end of his life: in Gethsemane, "Father, your will be done"; on the Cross, "Father, into your hands I commend my spirit." In the light of the resurrection of Jesus, we know that God is utterly faithful, and it is this truth and reality that we make the foundation of a Christian marriage.

Faithfulness presupposes intelligent faith and there is a rich inheritance of Christianity upon which to draw to build a marriage. Your duty will be to embody its truth by the faithfulness of your lives and worship; and this is a key to a long and happy marriage that is also a blessing to others. You may be sure that if you let God be the foundation of your marriage, he will be with you "for better, for worse". The hallmark of a strong marriage is therefore unflinching trust, in God and in each other; and herein lies its true wealth, "for richer, for poorer".

When we think of God the Son, we see Jesus set before us in the Gospels in every aspect of his humanity—as a baby in the womb, as a child growing up, as a young person full of gifts and energy, as a wonderful human person, courageous, sensitive and faithful to the end. We think of his patience and humility, his love and kindness, his capacity to reach out and to forgive, the sheer generosity of his coming among us. The purpose of a Christian marriage is to enable us to grow into his likeness, and to learn what it truly means to love each other as Jesus loves us. The key to such love is its self-sacrificial character, and in that it expresses the nature of the love of God himself.

We note that the authority of Jesus lies behind every true marriage, which is intended to be a loving relationship between a man and a woman, entered into freely and equally, and intended for life within the will of God. We note also the great emphasis that Jesus gave to the significance of children at the heart of marriage and society, "for of such is the kingdom of God" (Mark 10:14). The commitment that we make in marriage, "in sickness and in health", is certainly tested by the demanding care of children. Such a commitment mirrors the compassionate commitment of Jesus to us, and through us to our families and friends; and to all those whom we are called to serve. In the workplace as well as in the home, you are called to be ambassadors of Christ, and for the values of his kingdom. To your children, and indeed to all children, we hope you are called to be true mirrors of the love of God.

When we think of God the Holy Spirit, we sense something mysterious and life-giving that lies at the heart of our existence. The Holy Spirit is God giving himself to us in our life and health, our happiness and opportunities, in each other; also in our prayers, and in the sacrament of the Eucharist; and in those who, by his grace, we hope, will emerge as children within your new family. Giving lies at the heart of the goodness of God, and everything that we have is his gift to us, it is never our possession. This is why possessiveness is a travesty of love, something that destroys relationships. In a new marriage, parents have to give away their children with grace, encouragement and confidence, and also with prayer.

In a marriage, when children appear on the scene, they are a trust from God, never to be possessed, but always to be loved and cherished. The great test of Christian giving within relationships is found in forgiving and in receiving forgiveness. At the heart of a marriage therefore, there must always be sincere and loving communication, so that forgiveness may be received and shared, and never taken for granted. For all of us, young and old, need to feel secure and truly loved for all our days, "until death do us part".

You are not alone in this great endeavour of marriage. Your parents and siblings, relatives and friends, and also the fellowship of the Christian Church, stand alongside you with their prayers, affection and support. Others too witness your commitment: the saints of God in heaven without whose prayers none of us would make much progress as Christians. The person who can help you most to create a Christian marriage is Mary, the holy Mother of the Lord, who with the support of Joseph created a stable and loving home for Jesus himself. His confidence that he could address God as his Father was nurtured by the way he grew up as a child calling Joseph, "*Abba*". His obedience to the will of God was nurtured by the loving example of his own mother, someone whom he acclaimed as a person who always did the will of God. You should place her prayer at the heart of your own lives, and of your marriage and family: "I am the servant of the Lord: may it be to me according to your word" (Luke 1:38). Make her prayer your own each day and as you come to receive Holy Communion. Listen carefully for the voice of Jesus in the Gospels, and you will discover that you are both being enfolded within her prayers, as you become drawn deeper within the eternal love of God, Father, Son and Holy Spirit.

3 3

Children at the Heart of God's Kingdom

Mark 9:30-7,42; 10:13-16

It is striking that Mark's Gospel records such emphatic teaching by Jesus about the importance of children, which is reiterated in the Gospels of Matthew (18:1-10; 19:13-15) and Luke (17:2; 18:15-17). It is in Matthew's Gospel that additional teaching is given by Jesus that each child has a guardian angel in heaven. The Church need look no further in order to condemn child abuse by anyone in society or in its midst, as this is the only occasion when Jesus spoke about hanging millstones around the necks of those who abuse children. It was clearly a problem in his day as it is in our own. Damage done to a child in this way can wreck their chance of a stable life and inhibit loving relationships from forming. It is also a direct assault upon God, in whose image and likeness each human child is made, and can prove a barrier to sensing the love of God as Father.

It is also interesting that children and young people make significant appearances in the Gospels. Jesus was clearly approachable by them and wished to be so. There was the youngster who offered his picnic in John's account of the Feeding of the Five Thousand (John 6:9); the rich young man challenged by Jesus in very personal terms that probably changed his life (Mark 10:17-22); and the teenager who stole into the Garden of Gethsemane and had a narrow escape (Mark 14:51-2), who may have been the first witness to the resurrection of Jesus (Mark 16:5f.). The compassion of Jesus towards children and their stricken parents is evident at the bedside of Jairus' daughter (Mark 5:22f.) and at the funeral of the only son of a widow (Luke 7:11-17). Quite a number of his miracles of healing were of other children, even those whom he never actually met (Mark 7:24-30; John 4:46-54). Perhaps most striking of all is his teaching that people should address God as Father—*Abba*—using the word a child would use to its parent.

"Our Father" gives the starting point for thinking about how Christians should relate to children, for we are each called as children of God to be true mirrors of the love of God as each child's Father. It is only on this pastoral basis that the baptism of children can proceed. Deep reflection about how Jesus conveyed the sense of God as his Father and ours (John 20:17) will guard us against using the authority of God as a weapon of moral blackmail in the upbringing of children. It will equally warn us against the modern error of presenting God as some kind of "sugar-daddy" who will always forgive people whatever they do. The challenge for parents, teachers, clergy and others engaged in the care of the young is to convey the sense of the friendship and care of God for each person as a loving demand on their allegiance that will give direction to their lives. To combine kindness with firmness, faithfulness with high standards, forgiveness with embracing love—this requires great maturity and wisdom. We have always to reflect carefully on how God as our Father treats us and then act accordingly.

We must also ensure that children and young people have an accurate knowledge and understanding of the Gospels, so that they can see in Jesus a role model as well as a friend. The fact that God became a human person in Jesus gives value to each stage of human life and development. The conception of Jesus in the womb of Mary is a standing reproach to the ease with which modern society tolerates high rates of abortion. The circumstances of his birth in poverty alert us to the fact that every child is of value, and that parents who are poor and struggling need special care and support. As a young family, his parents had to flee as refugees, and many children have to endure chronic insecurity in our own day as refugees. Jesus in the Temple asking questions alerts those teaching the young to listen to their wisdom and to actually answer their questions. His ability to teach and preach so effectively was clearly rooted in his own devout Jewish upbringing and education. His confidence that he could address God as *Abba*—"Father"—reflects directly on the example and love of his own parents, Mary and Joseph. Their example and his own experience probably lay behind his unequivocal teaching about marriage, as well as his teaching about the care of children. The human context for the teaching of Jesus is always important to consider.

All this raises the question about what we mean by a Christian education. The first thing to say is that it is not about manipulation or indoctrination; nor is it about inculcating fear and guilt, or intolerance. Christian belief can never be compelled, as compulsion is not God's way, and Jesus himself demonstrated this by the way in which he taught and answered questions. T. S. Eliot once defined Christian education as "teaching young people to think in informed Christian categories, while never trying to compel Christian belief". It is a tragedy today that many Christian parents do not give proper priority to ensuring that their children receive an effective religious formation and education. Modern schools cannot be relied upon to fill this gap. But at the most superficial level, if children are ignorant of Christianity, they remain ignorant as they visit art galleries and cathedrals. Christian faith has to be transmitted across generations if the Church is to survive and thrive. Not to understand your own religious inheritance precludes any informed sympathy for the religious beliefs of others.

What is the spirit and content of Christian education—in the home, in church, and in a Christian school? In John's Gospel, Jesus said that the Holy Spirit "will teach you all things . . . and guide you into all truth" (John 14:26; 16:13). These words govern the ethos of Christian education which should comprise prayer, worship and teaching. Prayer first, as from the beginning of its existence in the womb a child should be supported by loving prayer and then taught how to address God directly and simply. Time spent in prayer with a little child, as with a dying person, reveals the inner reality of the soul, shining like a hidden pearl of glory. When children are brought to church, they should experience genuine worship and not entertainment, as church buildings convey their own truth and holiness, to which children are often very sensitive, as they are to Christian art and music. Children also learn from example whether going to church regularly is a priority in the family. Children have the right to know about the history of Christianity in all its rich diversity, especially in their own country, and to be taught how to approach the Bible and read it intelligently, regularly and prayerfully. They need to know about the lives of saints; and they can benefit greatly from visits to monasteries and other historic centres of Christian life and culture, at home or abroad. They also need to sense that they are not alone as Christians in an increasingly ignorant secular environment, and this is particularly true when they go to secondary school, university and into employment away from home.

Underlying all care and education of the young is the simple fact that we are all children of God. Very often in moments of pastoral crisis or need, a priest can see clearly that the child remains at the heart of a person's identity and existence. In dealing with teenagers, it is helpful to reflect that God probably sees us all as spiritual adolescents, even though some adults seem to remain stuck in their development at times! This is why children and teenagers need special care and encouragement, so that in the midst of the turbulence of growing up they sense that they are still valued completely for the person that they are. The wisdom of St Bernard of Clairvaux remains a sure guide for adults and children alike, when he said that "life is given to us to learn how to love, and time is given to us in order to find God". In our care of the young, we have to be true partners with the Holy Spirit in the nurture of each unique child, who is made in God's image and likeness. This will only happen if we allow the Holy Spirit to lead us also into all truth as it is revealed in Jesus himself, who is the Way, the Truth and the Life (John 14:6).

3 4

The Fruit of Love

1 John 4:7–21

"God is love: a person who abides in love abides in God, and God abides in him" (1 John 4:15). There is no finer nor more lucid exposition of the meaning of Christianity than in the first letter of St John. It comes across with decisive freshness and force as the first example of Christian catechesis—systematic instruction for new converts in how to become truly Christian. At its heart lies a profound redefinition of the meaning of the word "love", demonstrating how the Greek word *agape* came to distil the heart of the Gospel and to determine the distinctive ethos of Christianity.

The writer addresses his readers and hearers as "beloved", as people who are called to love one another, for love flows from the heart of God. It distinguishes those who are truly God's children: "for everyone who truly loves is begotten of God and knows him". This is a statement of universal significance as it embraces all human beings. If they are loving people, whoever they are, their life has its tap-root in God himself, and in them God draws near. To behave in a way contrary to love, however, is to undermine the very essence of being human; it is to turn one's back on God, just as to turn away from light is to enter shadow and, in the end, darkness.

There is therefore an intimate relationship between loving God, knowing God and living in union with God, which the writer proceeds to examine. Firstly, how do we actually know that God is love? We may believe that God is the greatest being conceivable, whose existence is eternal, and whose nature is utterly good. But how can we be sure of his love towards us? It is only in Jesus Christ that we can be sure that God truly loves us. It is only by embracing his love, and being embraced by it, that we can truly live as human beings. Do not so many human problems have their root in a gnawing sense of not being truly loved?

Only God is able to reach human beings by his initiative of love revealed in Christ. Our love of him is our response to his love for us from the moment of our conception as human beings: as is said at Confirmation, "I have called you by name and made you my own." There is no way in which human beings, manipulated by evil, can ever destroy this love. It is, however, only this divine love that can redeem human beings from their destructive tendencies, which we call sin. This is why the Cross of Jesus stands at the heart of human history as its central reference point and ultimate truth. Confronted by Christ crucified, we either accept the love of God or we reject it; we either choose life or, in the end, death.

Divine love is overflowing in its generosity: "If God so loved us, we ought also to love one another." We see this in the way in which Jesus expanded the great commandment in the Old Testament to love God and our neighbour. He calls us to love others as he has loved us, by self-sacrifice and self-giving, by empathy and compassion. The test of whether we really embrace this pattern of divine love is whether we are prepared to love and, if possible, forgive our enemies, as Jesus did in his prayer for his tormentors while on the Cross.

It is only divine love that brings God's reality close to human beings, and one of the definitions of a Christian saint is someone who makes God close and real. "If we love one another, God abides in us and his love is being made perfect in us." These are extraordinary words. But they rest on the cardinal belief in the Bible that human beings are made in the image and likeness of God. Each human person in their individual uniqueness is called to reflect and express something true about the uniqueness of God.

A key word in this letter, as in the Fourth Gospel, is the verb "to abide". The writer of this letter proceeds to explain part of what this means. Firstly, it signifies the indwelling of the Holy Spirit in a human person, called and designed to become a sanctuary of the Holy Spirit. It is on the altar of the heart that the flame of the Spirit descends, as we abide in him through our prayers. Secondly, we abide in God when we profess our faith in Jesus Christ as God's Son, sent into the world to show us what God is truly like, and to redeem humanity by his death on the Cross. Thirdly, such faith leads us to true knowledge of God: "We know and have believed the love that God has towards us." In Christianity, faith is a matter of intelligent and loving trust, as in any true relationship. In our relationship with God, to know him is to love him, and to love him is to know him.

Love of God is our only foundation for confidence in eternal life, for "perfect love casts out fear". This comes very close indeed to the heart of God's mission in Christ to rescue humanity: "Peace be with you—it is I myself: do not be afraid!" (John 6:20). Only a loving relationship with a loving God can enable us to appear in his presence at the moment of judgement after our lives end. Divine love is thus a perfecting process throughout our lives, a continual remaking of human life and love, a deepening of sensibility and understanding, and an enlarging of compassion and vision. "We love God because he first loved us." As St Bonaventure said: "Lord, I came forth from Thee, Most High; I come back to Thee, Most High; and only through Thee, Most High."

The practical test of our love, however, is always how we relate to other people: "for a person who does not love his brother or sister whom he can see can hardly love God whom he has not seen". Thus, as parents and teachers, godparents and grandparents, clergy and religious, we are each called to be clear mirrors of God's love to the children and young people in our care. As carers, personal or professional, we are called to show genuine compassion and understanding to all who need our help; and tolerance, forgiveness and understanding are the foundations of Christian friendship. As a society, our laws should enable people to live stable lives with their families, without fear. Divine love is therefore something utterly practical if its spiritual reality is rooted deeply within our hearts, as individual Christians and as the Church. For as Jesus said, "I have come that they may have life—life in all its fullness" (John 10:10).

3 5

Enfolded in Love

A sermon for Trinity-tide

"May the grace of the Lord Jesus Christ, and the love of God, and the communion of the Holy Spirit be with you all" (2 Corinthians 13:14). These lovely words of Paul at the end of his second letter to the church in Corinth have become a favourite prayer for private and public use. They alert us to the fact that belief in God the Trinity is implicit in the language of prayer that emerges throughout the New Testament, and especially in the various letters. This is because Christian belief in the Trinity is not a theory about God, nor the result of human reflection or speculation. Those who wrote the New Testament were all devout Jews who believed profoundly in one invisible God, who had revealed himself in history to their ancestors by his Name, given to Moses at the Burning Bush, and also as Divine Wisdom.

What is distinctive about New Testament belief is that through the person of Jesus Christ, three divine persons become discernible within the Christian experience of the love of God. At the heart of the Fourth Gospel, Jesus says: "I will pray the Father, and he will give you another Comforter to be with you forever.... If a person loves me, he will keep my word; and my Father will love him, and we will come to him and make our dwelling with him.... The Comforter, the Holy Spirit, whom the Father will send in my Name, he will teach you all things, and call to remembrance all that I have said unto you" (John 14:16,23,26). These words intimate the profound mystery of God as the Trinity of Father, Son and Holy Spirit. They also reveal the fact that human beings are designed to be able to receive and relate to this self-revelation of God himself. Thus, the end of Matthew's Gospel contains the command of

Jesus to baptize people "in the Name of the Father, and of the Son, and of the Holy Spirit" (Matthew 28:19).

How should Christians think about the Trinity? These words of the fourth evangelist give us a clue: "God so loved the world that he gave his only begotten Son, that whoever believes in him should not perish, but should have eternal life" (John 3:16). The key phrase is "so loved". Divine love is the outpouring of divine goodness. The essential goodness of God is the heart of his unity and uniqueness. It is the nature of goodness to find gratuitous expression in creation; and it is the nature of love to be poured out in relationships. A unity of goodness and love: this is at the heart of what Christians believe about the nature of God. They share this belief with Jews and Muslims; but the person of Jesus opens new vistas into the significance of God's goodness and love and therefore the nature of his uniqueness.

In human life, the highest that any person can give is himself or herself. We see this in a Christian marriage between a man and woman, which is a free but binding union, a covenant that is intended to last for life. The key to a lasting marriage is an equal and sustained outpouring of mutual love, given, valued and received, whose supreme expression is patience, faithfulness and forgiveness. Its fruit is found in children, whose procreation and nurture are the principal reason for Christian marriage. Children flourish when they are loved fully and equally by both parents together. From such a marriage and family life, love also flows out into the community, to friends and neighbours. This is why marriage stands at the heart of Christianity and its ethics, and the family is at the heart of the Church. For Christian marriage mirrors and mediates something profound about the nature of God; and its most important function is to mirror and mediate the love of God to children, who are entrusted by God to human care.

God gives himself in the person of Jesus for our redemption because he has given himself eternally to his Son. The Son mirrors the life-giving capacity of God, and this finds expression in the Holy Spirit, who is the beloved bond and expression of equal love between the Father and the Son. The communion of the Father, the Son and the Holy Spirit is a communion of overflowing love that is self-giving and self-sacrificing; and this is revealed supremely to human beings on the Cross.

"God so loved the world that he gave his only Son." Why? "So that whoever believes in him might not perish but have eternal life." This is the heart of the Gospel, and it addresses all human beings as God's children. This is also the measure of the essential goodness of God himself. For God's intention from the beginning was, and is, to create human beings in his own image and likeness (Genesis 1:26), and to restore them to become "sanctuaries of the Holy Spirit" (1 Corinthians 6:19). Thus, belief in the Trinity is the key to understanding the nature and destiny of each unique human being as a person loved by God, redeemed by his Son, and transformed by the Holy Spirit. So "may the grace of the Lord Jesus Christ, the love of God, and the communion of the Holy Spirit enfold us all" (2 Corinthians 13:14) within the Trinity of God himself forever.

In this prayer, Alcuin, who lived in the eighth century, conveys to us something of this profound vision of the dynamic love that is within God, Father, Son and Holy Spirit:

> Be present, O true Light, the Father who is God Almighty.
> Be present, O Light from Light, the Word and Son of God.
> Be present, O Holy Spirit, the bond of loving union
>   between the Father and the Son.
> Be present, One Almighty God, Father, Son, and Holy Spirit.
> Teach us faith, awaken hope, and fill us with your love.
> Give us the purity that comes from you and cannot come from us.
> For you are love, grace and communion:
> God is love, Christ is grace, and the Holy Spirit is communion.
> The true Light, true Light from true Light, and the Illuminator;
> The fountain, the river and the refreshing stream:
> Living life, Life from the Living One, Life-giver to the living.
> The true Father, truth in the Son, and in the Holy Spirit:
>   O blessed Trinity.

3 6

The Spirit of Prayer

Philippians 1:1–11

Grace to you and peace from God our Father and from the Lord Jesus Christ

Paul's letters contain significant witness to his own life of prayer, and some of his language has passed into the liturgy and worship of the Church. His letter to the Philippians reveals how deeply he felt towards the Christians in that city, whose faith he had kindled and then nurtured over many years. His first visit there is recorded in striking detail in the Acts of the Apostles, and his rapport with them remained close as they generously supported his missionary activities. Philippi remained an important Christian centre into the fourth and later centuries, and its ruins today contain two major basilican churches, and one which is octagonal in the midst of a complete church centre, comprising a bishop's residence, a hostel and a baptistry. Most moving of all, perhaps, is the rather crude mosaic that records how the bishop Porphyrios dedicated the first church to St Paul there, building it around AD 325, very soon after the persecution of Christians was stopped by the Roman emperor Constantine, and churches could be openly constructed. In the Middle Ages, Paul was often referred to as "the Apostle", such was his authority as a spiritual teacher of prayer.

I thank my God by always remembering you

Paul begins his prayer for those who will read and hear his letter by joining together the key elements of Christian prayer—thanksgiving and remembrance. The Eucharist itself is precisely that: an act of remembrance and thanksgiving, modelled on Jewish practice each Sabbath and pre-eminently at Passover. To remember in this way is to join together the present and the past within the eternal purpose of God. It is also to join ourselves with others within the eternal love of God.

I always pray for you all with a spirit of joy

It is fundamental to Christian compassion faithfully to remember others in our prayers. Prayer for others should be a duty, but it is also a joy: duty is the husk of the nut, but joy is its inner life and fruit. We pray for others because we love and care for them, however we may relate to them. Intercession for others does not discriminate, for all are children of the same heavenly Father. Such prayer expresses a proper valuing of others, even of enemies.

I value your fellowship in furthering the Gospel from your beginning until now

The key word here is fellowship—in Greek *koinonia*. In the light of the Acts of the Apostles, this signifies an active partnership of Christians in mission with the Holy Spirit. It also signifies close and loving collaboration and communication between Christians, near and far, which is the bond of love and of a common vision. It is also a commitment to mutual encouragement and practical support. One of the privileges of travelling to churches abroad is to sense the reality of this *koinonia*—this fellowship in the Gospel.

I am confident that God who began a good work among you will perfect it in the day of Jesus Christ

In these words, Paul reveals the spirit and expectation of Christian prayer, rooted in a confident trust in God. Such faith discerns and responds to the continual perfecting work of God's grace in the life of each person who puts their trust in him. Christian life is a continual perfecting, not in the sense of perfectionism or being perfect, but rather as a tiny child unfolds by growing up as a beautiful work of art designed by God to express his image and likeness. Prayer therefore seeks to affirm this process of divine remaking and perfecting with all patience and love, confident in the providential purpose of God for each person.

It is entirely right for me to have you in my heart in this way as partakers with me of divine grace

To pray for others is to bear them in our hearts in the presence of God. We may not always know how we should pray for them, but such prayer respects and is sensitive to their deepest needs and sustains and values their integrity as children of a loving God. As St Gregory the Great once said to the Archbishop of Alexandria, when reporting about the progress of St Augustine's mission to the English: "Your good deeds are evident where you are, but your prayers reach where you cannot be." Prayer for others unites us with them, as it expresses our love for them within the love of God for them.

God himself knows how I long for you all with the tender compassion of Christ

Paul was a deeply emotional person, who felt a keen bond of love and responsibility towards those whom he evangelized. His letters came to be regarded as sacramental signs of his apostolic devotion. He sensed the deep affinity created between himself and his fellow Christians, even though he was often distant from them physically. Christian prayer is therefore a supreme work of compassion for others, near and far, and this is why intercession is so central in Christian worship.

I pray that your love may abound more and more in knowledge and discernment

"Life is given that we may learn how to love." These words of St Bernard put the whole of Christian life into a positive and purposeful perspective. As we pray for others, so our capacity for love grows. As we pray alongside the Holy Spirit within us, we grow in discernment and knowledge, in Christian wisdom. We begin to see others with the eyes of Christ. We sense and respect their unique value to God who made them. We encourage with loving patience the emerging fruits of the Holy Spirit within them. We place their lives as well as our own into the loving hands of God our heavenly Father, by praying "Thy will be done" in them as well as in ourselves. Paul prays elsewhere that Christ may be formed within those to whom he is writing and for whom he prays so earnestly.

May you discern what is excellent and become truly sincere in the light of the judgement of Christ

The heart of Christian prayer is worship; and the foundation of true worship is sincerity as the love of God and love for others goes hand in hand. The life of prayer deepens and strengthens our inner moral integrity because it is the path of true love for others, whose servants we are. Prayer is never about manipulation or possession of others. Instead, it is governed by a sense of responsibility and accountability for how we pray and for how we live.

May you be filled with the fruits of righteousness from Jesus Christ to the glory and praise of God

Christians never pray alone as our prayer is always part of something much bigger and deeper than ourselves, a true *koinonia* rooted in the eternal love and purpose of God the Trinity. Our private prayer prepares us for public worship, which itself derives vigour from how Christians pray at home each day of the week. There is no end to prayer inasmuch as it is a lifetime's art, a continual education by the Holy Spirit as he leads us into all truth. There is no limit either to the human capacity to share in the eternal love of God. This is our destiny and also our joy. Fruit signifies divine life within us: it is not something that we achieve, or for which we can take any credit. We simply have to pray to our Lord each day, "Thy will be done" in me, making as our own the prayer of the Blessed Virgin Mary: "Behold, I am the servant of the Lord: may it be to me according to your word" (Luke 1:38).

3 7

Faith, Hope and Love in the Face of Death

A sermon for All Souls Day

Jesus said to Martha, "I am the resurrection and the life: a person who believes in me, even if they die, shall live; and whoever believes in me shall never die. Do you believe this?" (John 11:25-6). There is no more daunting a moment for a priest than beginning a Christian funeral service with these words. He or she is addressed by the same challenge of Jesus, "Do you believe this?", as are the bereaved relatives coming into church or crematorium chapel. Faith, hope and love are put to the sternest test when confronted by the inevitable reality of death. As Socrates said long ago when facing his own death by execution, to fear death is to claim some knowledge of what happens. In his day, as he said, no-one could know whether death was the ultimate blessing or the gateway to oblivion. The resurrection of Jesus is the foundation of Christian faith, hope and love because now to some extent we do know how to confront death.

In the Gospels, the word "faith" also means "trust", as can be seen in the dialogue in John 11 between Jesus and Martha when confronted by the death of Lazarus. Her faith and that of her sister Mary was sorely strained by the fact that Jesus had delayed coming to see them in their loss, even though he loved them dearly. After four days, the death of Lazarus was final and the situation was hopeless. "If only you had been here!" These harrowing words spring to the lips of so many people when a person dies. "If only . . . " In this case, "If only you had been here, my brother would not have died." Yet in the face of such grief, her hope still sprang eternal, being rooted in her relationship with Jesus: "But even now I know that whatever you ask of God, God will give you." Her human faith at another level, however, was shattered by the stark reality of death—an abstract Jewish religious belief in resurrection at the last day brought her no comfort. Nor can empty platitudes help anyone today.

Only trust in Jesus rescued Martha from her despair: "I do believe that you are the Christ, the Son of God, who has come into the world." Here we have the heart of the Gospel affirmed as her relationship with Jesus survived its ultimate test. Her example and response guide each one of us when confronted by the death of someone we love, for it is in the darkness that the light of Christ shines clearest. "Yea, though I walk through the valley of the dark shadow of death, I will fear no evil: for you are with me" (Psalm 23:4). Martha was able to speak words of daring hope, secretly and under her breath, to her grieving sister, Mary: "The Master is here and he is calling for you." Mary's grief broke the heart of Jesus and he wept. It provoked an acute crisis, for Jesus knew that raising Lazarus from death would seal his own fate.

Hope cannot be simply wishful or sentimental thinking, even though such aspirations find expression in some secular readings and poems used at funerals. Christian hope has its anchor in reason, inasmuch as it is not unreasonable, even if it cannot be proved, to believe that human life is not destroyed utterly by death. As Jesus and many others have pointed out, "living through dying" is built into the natural world, often on an annual cycle, for out of death and decay springs new life. Moreover, is it likely that human beings, made in the image and likeness of God, are ultimately expendable and that their personal life has no meaning, being merely the product of random chance and evolutionary development? This is a serious question that Christianity addresses with cautious confidence. We believe that human life in this world does have a purpose and meaning: for as St Bernard once said, "Life is given to us to learn how to love, and time is given to us so that we may find God." This means, among other things, that it is quite reasonable to believe that human lives and their loving relationships find their fulfilment beyond this life, just as the life of a foetus in the womb passes from that existence to emerge into the fullness of life and love as a human child.

The only basis for Christian hope is the relationship that we have with God himself in this life; and his love for us is the sole ground for our hope—for ourselves and for others whom we love. This deep and instinctive human hope is closely related to our experience of love. When someone dies, we face the perplexing situation of love being, as it were, suspended. We still love and cherish the person, but we must at a deep level let them go. We remember them with affection and gratitude, as we do today and each year; and their memory is a living part of our life, and still a wellspring of love. But we have to entrust them to God who made them and who loves them. This is why the grief of Jesus at the tomb of Lazarus is so significant and life-giving: "Jesus wept." He reveals the deep empathy that is rooted in the heart of God. The Greek text says that Jesus was rocked to the core. Those standing by said, "Behold, how he loved him!" The resurrection of Lazarus, four days dead and decaying, was a shattering experience for all concerned. It literally altered human history forever, for those with eyes to see and hearts to believe. It caused an acute crisis for the religious authorities in Jerusalem, putting Jesus and Lazarus at risk. The human command, "Loose him and let him go!", completed the divine command, "Lazarus, come forth!"

The prophetic words of Jesus himself thus came true: "The hour approaches and it has already struck when the dead shall hear the voice of the Son of God, and those who hear it will live" (John 5:25). Christian faith, hope and love in the face of death are underpinned by the resurrection of Jesus himself: "Do not be afraid: I am the first and the last, the Living One. I became dead, and behold I am alive for evermore; and I have the keys of death and the underworld" (Revelation 1:17–18). With this promise, the inevitable moment of death that confronts each one of us, as it did Martha and Mary long ago, becomes the threshold of eternal life and love, the supreme affirmation of faith, hope and love, placing our lives, and the lives of those whom we love but see no longer, where they belong—into the hands of the living and loving God, who comes to meet us there at the empty tomb in the risen person of Jesus himself.

PART 6

Contemplative Worship

3 8

Divine Ascent

A sermon for Ascensiontide

1 John 5

The call of Jesus to "Follow me!" leads us from the Sea of Galilee, up the mountain of Transfiguration, into the Garden of Gethsemane, and finally onto Calvary itself, before we hear his momentous words after his resurrection: "I ascend to my Father and your Father, to my God and your God" (John 20:17). What is the nature and meaning of this divine ascent? The final chapter of the first letter of John gives us an outline of how we may ascend to God by following the steps of Jesus himself.

Faith in Jesus Christ is the key. It means active trust in God as he comes to us in Jesus. It means accepting and willing the inner transformation of our lives by the love of God poured into our hearts. Love of Jesus leads us deeper into love of his Father; love of God the Father points us further into the mystery of Christ. We are called to become enfolded within the love that flows between the Father and the Son. In the process, we become more truly children of God, made like Christ, because we willingly and gladly accept the demands of divine love within our lives and relationships. God's commandments are not alien to our true nature because love is the basis of our affinity to God, and also of his affinity to us, who are made in his image and likeness. Our willing obedience is the sign of our loving relationship with God himself.

Faith in Christ enables us to see things and people with new eyes, to understand the moral and spiritual conflict that there is in the world, and to appreciate more fully the significance of the choices that we are called to make as Christians. We pray to the Holy Spirit to "enable with perpetual light the dullness of our blinded sight". Just as a scientist has to look deeply into the structure of created reality, often by demanding and arduous research, so we are called to look more deeply into the structure of spiritual reality, to learn how to acquire "the mind of Christ" and to see others in the light of God's love for them as well as for ourselves.

At the heart of reality, at the centre of human history, stands the mystery of the Cross: for Jesus "came by water and blood". The fourth evangelist witnessed the outpouring of water and blood from the side of Christ as he hung dead on the Cross (John 19:34). What does this signify? Part of its meaning is of course the graphic consequence of dying such a terrible death, leading to heart rupture. Part of its meaning is the tragic helplessness of Jesus, the stark reality of his suffering and dying. Part of its meaning also exposes the heart of God himself, the Creator of the world and the Father of humanity, who has to endure the grim despoliation of creation and of so many human beings by the cruelty engendered by evil intending to spite God himself. How can a Christian contemplate this abyss of divine suffering and love without being overwhelmed?

"It is the Spirit that bears witness, because the Spirit is truth." Only as a person is deeply enfolded within the love that flows between the Father, the Son and the Holy Spirit can the mystery of the Cross of Jesus be borne. This is why in certain Latin versions of this passage there is an explicit reference to the Trinity itself, inserted as a gloss. As Jesus said to his disciples: "it is the Spirit that gives life ... the words that I have spoken to you are spirit and life" (John 6:63).

"Water, blood and Spirit"—these together bear witness to and convey to us the reality of eternal life that God offers to everyone who puts their trust in Jesus and truly loves him as God's Son; for "God has given us eternal life, and this life is in his Son." The two basic sacraments of the Christian Church rest upon this foundation: the water of Baptism that mediates the coming of the Holy Spirit; and the bread and wine of Holy Communion that signify and mediate the Body and Blood of Christ. As we receive these sacraments, so our lives begin to change, as divine life and love courses through our veins and takes up residence within our hearts. "A person who has the Son has this life" because Christ is dwelling within us by his Holy Spirit. Just as the lips of the prophet Isaiah were cleansed by allowing the angel to touch his tongue with a living, burning coal taken from the heavenly altar of God (Isaiah 6:6–7), so we have to accept the costly grace of Holy Communion, filled as it is with the invisible fire of the Holy Spirit.

Contemplation of the mystery of the Cross, mediated to us each week in Holy Communion, also enables us to enter within the stream of loving intercession that flows from Jesus as God's Son to the Father himself. The writer of the letter to the Hebrews asserts that Jesus "is able to save to the uttermost those that draw near to God through him, for he ever lives to make intercession for them" (Hebrews 7:25). The writer of the first letter of John encourages Christians to approach God with humble boldness, as children would speak to their own father, indeed as Jesus himself prayed—"*Abba*: father!" The heart of his relationship with his Father was enshrined in his words in the Lord's Prayer that culminate in "Thy will be done." So "if we ask anything according to his will, he hears us."

Discerning what is the will of God in any situation is the test of our Christian faith and prayer. It will never be put to the test in a more demanding way than when we find ourselves compelled to pray for others, who may be in dire need or spiritual danger, including our enemies and those who hate us. As Jesus said, and did: "love your enemies and pray for your persecutors" (Matthew 5:44). Can we pray in this way? We have to let the Spirit of Christ pray within us, joining our imperfect prayer to his.

The goal of our ascent to God is following Jesus, who is the way, the truth and the life (John 14:6), and it is summed up by the writer of the first letter of John in his concluding words: "We know that we are of God; . . . and we also know that the Son of God has come and given us true understanding, so that we may know him that is true, and be within him that is true, even his Son, Jesus Christ: for this is the true God and this is eternal life."

3 9

The Spirit of the Eucharist

Luke 24:36–48; 1 John 3:1–7

It is striking that in all the Gospels the reality of the resurrection of Jesus was received and mediated through existing relationships and friendships. It was the genius of the writer of John's Gospel to convey the full force of this with his moving descriptions of how Mary Magdalene encountered Jesus by the tomb; of how Thomas asked the question that every subsequent generation of Christians would ask; and of how Peter was restored in his relationship with Jesus, whom in a humiliating panic he had denied. In each case, it was a relationship restored and a friendship deepened; and the genius and authority of this Gospel writer rested upon his own intimate friendship with Jesus. The enigmatic short ending of Mark also presupposes existing relationships, for the young man in the empty tomb was probably not a complete stranger to the frightened women, even if his identity later remained hidden, perhaps for his own safety. Matthew's account is perhaps the least obviously personal; but there could be no recognition of Jesus alive except by those who actually knew him. Their testimony and their friendships remain the human foundation for Christian belief in the resurrection of Jesus.

Luke's Gospel rests upon close personal memories within the Jerusalem church and probably within the close family of Jesus himself, if Cleopas in Luke 24 was in fact his uncle, being the husband of Mary, who was the sister of the mother of Jesus (John 19:25). Luke's account is very close to John's Gospel in many respects. Jesus greeted his disciples with the traditional greeting, "Peace be with you!" These words now took on a deeper meaning, however, for "Christ is our peace" (Ephesians

2:14), and his healing peace springs from his saving death on the Cross for our redemption.

Jesus made himself known as a real person, which entailed having a human body that could be embraced and touched: "The Word became flesh" (John 1:14), so that "that which was from the beginning, that we have heard and seen with our own eyes, and that our hands have handled is the Word of Life" (1 John 1:1). Jesus said to his disciples, "It is I myself." But the test of the reality of his risen presence was the livid marks of crucifixion in his hands, feet and side. The other test of his reality was his sitting down to eat with them. "Do you have anything here to eat?" The reality of their friendship with him and with each other was expressed in their sharing a common meal. This is also apparent in the account at the end of John's Gospel in Chapter 21. The implication of this truth is a major theme in the preceding story in Luke 24 about how the disciples in Emmaus encountered Jesus. As their guest took the bread to bless and break it, they recognized who it was—Jesus himself.

The context for their acceptance of the resurrection of Jesus also lay in a deeper understanding of Scripture. The resurrection of Jesus was not a complete bolt from the blue, inasmuch as in his own teaching he had indicated it as the outcome of his own predicted suffering, even though they did not understand him at the time. "He opened their minds that they might now understand the Scriptures." The suffering and death of the Servant of God was implicit in Scripture—notably in some of the psalms, for example Psalm 22, and in Isaiah 53; or in the Lamentations of Jeremiah. Inherent too in Scripture was the global mission of the Messiah, the outpouring of the love of God for the whole world: "You are now the witnesses of these things." Their testimony now constitutes the New Testament.

"That which we have seen and heard we declare unto you, so that you may have fellowship with us. Indeed, our fellowship (or communion) is with the Father and with his Son, Jesus Christ" (1 John 1:3). Here is the key word—communion (in Greek: *koinonia*)—that connects our celebration of Holy Communion each week with the events and experience of the first Easter. We are called to become the friends of God in Jesus Christ, for he says to us also, "I have called you friends" (John 15:15). If we are truly friends of Jesus, we become friends of each other in the Church in a new relationship of deep communion that transcends all human differences and distinctions. In the words of Paul to the Colossians, "You have put on a new humanity, which is being renewed in knowledge after the image of him who created it: for here there can no longer be Greek and Jew, circumcised and uncircumcised, barbarian or Scythian, slave nor free; for Christ is all and in all" (Colossians 3:10–11).

This is why there is only one Eucharist at the heart of the Church because it is only through receiving Holy Communion that Christians become part of the Body of Christ. The Eucharist defines the place and nature of the Christian Church, and there should be no barriers to receiving communion if people have been baptized into Christ. At the altar rail, all are equal as children of God and brothers and sisters of Jesus Christ. By this means, division and hostility are overcome and human nature is actually made new by the indwelling of the Holy Spirit. The Christian Church was from the first a multi-racial organization gathered around the shared meal of the Eucharist, and this remains true today.

This is why Christians should give absolute priority to receiving Holy Communion regularly and making regular worship in church the focus of their lives. You cannot be a Christian in isolation, nor should you take the availability of the sacrament for granted. Our worship has to rest upon deep conviction and not degenerate into a matter of mere convenience. Going to church should not be regarded as one leisure option to compete with others. How far do we actually value receiving Holy Communion? The events of the past year of lockdowns, when receiving the sacrament has been sadly disrupted, should bring this question into sharp focus for us all.

We are all called to be disciples of Jesus Christ. Is our life being "renewed in knowledge"? If the earliest disciples had to see Christ in a new light and read the Scriptures afresh in that light, how about us? Diligent daily prayer coupled with reading the Gospels is the essential foundation of Christian life. We are called to love God with all our mind as well as our heart, and it is in prayerful dialogue with the Bible that we come to understand the mind of God as revealed in Jesus Christ. Christians are called to life-long learning, and this is why we have readings at the Eucharist that are drawn from the Old and New Testaments, including the poetry of the psalms, which were the prayers of Jesus himself. As we hear them in the light of his death and resurrection, we prepare ourselves to receive Holy Communion.

The words of this epistle set before each one of us a commanding goal: "Behold, what manner of love the Father has bestowed upon us that we should be called the children of God: and such indeed we are.... Beloved, we are already children of God, though it is not yet revealed what we shall be. But we do know that when he is revealed, we shall be like him: for we shall see him as he is." This is our vocation—to become truly Christ-like people, true children of God in whose image and likeness we have each been created. This is why coming to Holy Communion is indeed "our duty and our joy".

4 0

Receiving Holy Communion

"As often as you eat this bread and drink this cup, you proclaim the Lord's death until he comes" (1 Corinthians 11:26). So, every time you come to Holy Communion you take part in something which has occurred at the heart of the Church's life since the beginning, as these words of St Paul indicate. Indeed, one way of defining the nature of the Christian Church is by its regular celebration of the Eucharist; and nothing is more moving than to attend a service of Holy Communion in a church far from home, and to sense that we are part of the one Body of Christ.

Over the last year, because of various lockdowns, the opportunity to receive Holy Communion regularly has been denied to many people, in this country and abroad, because of the closure of churches during the pandemic. This is a serious loss, even if it has been prompted by a health emergency, whose full impact at the beginning could not be accurately assessed. Now, however, there is no impediment to receiving Holy Communion regularly and as a priority; and perhaps its enforced absence will make us all take the sacrament more seriously and less for granted. How and why should we come regularly to Holy Communion?

Firstly, because in Holy Communion Christians sense the presence of the risen Christ, even as he appeared to his first disciples in the context of their shared meals. Jesus said, "Where two or three are gathered together in my Name, there am I in their midst" (Matthew 18:20). Do we wish to meet him?

Secondly, because Holy Communion enables us to receive the Bread of Life, which is Christ himself. He says, "I am the Bread of Life ... the Living Bread which came down from heaven, so that whoever eats this bread shall live forever" (John 6:51). Holy Communion deepens our relationship with Christ. Receiving Holy Communion regularly also heals us from the inroads of sin. It is medicine as well as food for our souls.

Thirdly, the celebration of Holy Communion reminds us not to take the grace of God for granted, and to remember that divine forgiveness flows into our lives at great cost: for Jesus said, "This is my body that is given up for you" (Luke 22:19). Coming to Holy Communion brings us each week to the foot of the Cross of Calvary, to the one, true and perfect sacrifice made once for all for the forgiveness of our sins.

Fourthly, receiving Holy Communion should always be preceded by careful and prayerful preparation, perhaps by reading the passages from the Bible that will be used at the next service. There should be nothing casual about how we come to communion, and it should always be a matter of conviction and priority, and never of mere convenience.

Fifthly, by receiving Holy Communion we become living members of the Body of Christ, the Church. We are at one with Christians of every church and in every part of the world. This is why we pray each week for the life of the worldwide Church; and also why, as Anglicans, we welcome to Holy Communion all baptized Christians who would normally receive communion in their own churches. In welcoming the stranger and visitor to Holy Communion, we are welcoming Jesus himself, who said, "inasmuch as you did this to one of the least of my brethren, you did it to me" (Matthew 25:40).

Sixthly, in Holy Communion we pray for the life of the world, for those in government, for the poor and the sick, the afflicted and the bereaved; and we also commemorate those who have died. We begin to look at others with the eyes of Christ and to care for them with his compassion. The sacrament can heal our lives and the lives of others; it can also help bring peace and reconciliation to our world. For Jesus said: "I have come that they may have life, life in all its fullness" (John 10:10).

Finally, when we stand before the altar at Holy Communion, we join with the priest in the eternal worship of heaven: "Holy, Holy, Holy! Lord God of hosts. Heaven and earth are full of Thy glory! Glory be to Thee, O Lord Most High. Blessed is he that cometh in the Name of the Lord. Hosanna in the Highest!" In these words, we acclaim the coming and presence of the Lord Jesus Christ who said, "Behold, I am making all things new" (Revelation 21:5).

Here is an Anglo-Saxon prayer of preparation for receiving Holy Communion:

> Lord Jesus Christ, the Way, the Truth and the Life: we seek eternal life that you may make us your friends. You came from heaven to pour life into the world; we know you to be the Bread of Life, the loving bond of human hearts. Someone who comes to you will never suffer hunger; someone who believes in you will never thirst. For you are the true bread, your flesh is all-powerful, and your blood, Jesus, is the true drink of the faithful. By this mystery you redeem us from death, so that we may live in you, Lord, more securely and wisely. We therefore pray you to make us worthy to share in this holy mystery to the praise of your Name.
>
> You, Christ, are our teacher to whom we draw near in love; may we be filled with your grace and assistance by this sacrament. May your love be the foundation of our hearts and minds, so that we may be kindled with brotherly affection. Grant us peace of soul and mind always, for you are our true peace: preserve us in it, O God. Where there is peace, you yourself draw near; where you are, may your own be also. Come to us, O Lord, and possess us with joy, so that we may become temples for your Holy Spirit. Amen.
>
> *From the ninth-century Nunnaminster Codex*

4 1

The Bread of Life

A sermon for Lammastide

Lammas Day falls on 1 August each year according to the *Book of Common Prayer*, and it is the ancient forerunner of Harvest Festival, which in its present form is a late Victorian creation. It dates from Anglo-Saxon times, when it probably replaced an earlier pagan festival marking the beginning of harvest, which may have gone back to Neolithic times. Traditionally, a loaf of bread was blessed that was made from the first corn harvested and ground, such was their utter dependence on a reliable harvest each year at a time when it was so difficult to store food safely for any long period. Later in the Middle Ages it became associated with the feast of St Peter in Chains, a second commemoration of the apostle, remembering the time when he was miraculously delivered from prison in Jerusalem (Acts 12). Lammas is also associated with the Jewish offering of first-fruits in gratitude to God. Today, it provides a good opportunity to express support and appreciation to our farmers at the beginning of harvest, and to all those involved in the food industry. Like Harvest Festival itself, it challenges our attitudes and values towards the created world, upon which all human life depends.

This is because the fundamental principle enshrined in this ancient feast is that we should always offer the first and the best to God in humble gratitude for his gift of life to us and to the whole natural world. In the Old Testament, the first-born was offered to God, recalling how God gave Isaac back to Abraham as a sign of his covenant and promise. Samuel, John the Baptist and Jesus himself were all offered to God in this way as first-born male children. Today, we may express this profound truth in words taken from the Orthodox liturgy: "Thine own, of Thine own, for all and through all we offer Thee, O Lord." We should make this principle of offering the first and the best to God the basis of our lives as Christians, renewing our own self-offering to God each day in union with that of Jesus himself.

Bread forms a central symbol in the Bible, for both Jews and Christians. For Jews, the *Torah*—the Law of God—is often described as the Bread of God, or the Bread of Life. So, when Jesus called himself "the Bread of Life" he was expressing this deep Jewish belief now revealed and fulfilled in his own person, saying that "the Bread of God is that which comes down from heaven and gives life to the world" (John 6:33). Bread also features at the heart of the Lord's Prayer: "Give us this day our *daily* bread." The Greek word *epiousios* is a rare word, and it has a range of possible meanings. It can simply mean "daily" or "continual", and therefore sufficient for tomorrow too. It clearly means that which is necessary for existence; and it may express a prayer for the bread of God's kingdom to come: in Latin, it has been translated as *supersubstantialis*. In the early Christian *Didache* (8), the Lord's Prayer was closely associated with the Eucharist; and since the time of St Gregory the Great it has been placed immediately after the consecrating prayer in most Western rites.

This theme of bread is also picked up in the modern offertory prayer: "Blessed are you, Lord God of all creation, through your goodness we have this bread to offer, which earth has given and human hands have made: may it become for us the Bread of Life." The simple prayer, "Give us today our daily bread", is in fact the pivot of Christian social ethics. For bread is never just for personal use: it is to be shared by all; and it calls to mind keenly those who are hungry and poor. The very making of bread depends upon social and economic co-operation, and at the present time the conflict in Ukraine is causing a massive food crisis in poorer countries across the world. This is why Christians should say grace before every meal, and teach their children to do so as well: "We bless Thee, O Lord, for these and all Thy gifts to us, through Jesus Christ our Lord: always make us mindful of the needs of others." Such a regular daily prayer of gratitude protects us and our families from ever taking food for granted, let alone wasting it. The meaning of the word "Eucharist" is thanksgiving, and this is the distinctive ethos of all Christian life and worship.

Some of the parables of Jesus alert us to the way in which the making of bread can convey truth about the coming of God's kingdom into our lives. "The kingdom of heaven is like leaven, or yeast, which a woman took and hid within three measures of meal, until it was all leavened" (Matthew 13:33). The parable of the Sower speaks about the quality or otherwise of grain offered to God as the harvester. St Paul speaks about the fruits of the Spirit, generated within our lives by the grace of God, if we so permit it. The mingling of yeast with flour is a potent symbol of the irreversible union between God and human nature expressed in the person of Jesus for the redemption of humanity. The grinding of flour, stripping it of all its external matter, is a powerful symbol of the ascetic life of Christianity, setting aside all that would encumber the life of God's Spirit within us. Salt and oil are added to the dough, and both are Gospel symbols that express the nearness and life-giving power of God's kingdom and his Spirit. Bread dough must be energetically stretched, and then hidden in a dark place, before being roasted in a hot oven. Indeed, "It is a fearful thing to fall into the hands of the living God" (Hebrews 10:31). But no baking—no bread!

St Augustine once said that Christians see set before them on the altar that which they are called to become. We express this in words said by a priest before Holy Communion: "We break this Bread to share in the Body of Christ: though we are many, we are one Body, for we all share in the one Bread." For in the words of St Paul, "The bread that we break, is it not a communion in the Body of Christ?" (1 Corinthians 10:16–17). Each time we approach the sacrament, therefore, we should remember that when God so loved the world that he gave his only Son, he gave only his best—himself in human form, for our redemption and to share in his own eternal life and love. This is the promise of Jesus to all who receive him in love: "I am the living bread which came down from heaven; and if anyone eats of this bread, he will live forever: for the bread that I will give is my flesh, for the life of the world" (John 6:51); for "Christ has been raised from the dead, the first-fruits of those who are asleep" (1 Corinthians 15:20).

4 2

Encountering Silence

A sermon in preparation for Lent

One of the most striking things about worshipping with the Carthusians is the way in which their liturgy is steeped in silence as the active counterpoint to words. Their style of worship is nine hundred years old, well-honed within their secluded way of life. At the Eucharist, a profound silence follows the Gospel reading and precedes receiving communion. In the office of the night, darkness and silence envelop the recitation of the psalms. Why is silence so important in Christian worship?

Silence on a mountain-top, silence by the sea, or in a forest, or in the depths of the desert—in such moments people often sense the reality of God. This can also be true in certain churches and cathedrals; and it is striking too on Mount Athos, which is a natural and worshipping environment of great beauty that has been devoted to Christian prayer for over a thousand years. One of the most thought-provoking sentences in the book of Revelation says that "there was silence in heaven for about half an hour" (Revelation 8:1). What can this enigmatic statement mean?

Sometimes at Advent or Christmas, these beautiful words are heard from the book of Wisdom: "When all things were lying in peace and silence, and night in her swift course was half spent, your all-powerful Word leapt from your royal throne in heaven" (Wisdom 18:14–15). The sense that the Word of God emerges from silence has its root in the Hebrew word *dabar*. This means something that God conceives, utters and achieves by his Word: we have a relic of this in the idea of a magic spell. In Jesus Christ, God's Word was fully expressed in a human person, made in the true image and likeness of God, and filled by God's Word, who is the true Image and Likeness of God.

Towering above the ancient monastery of St Catherine are the red granite mountains of Sinai, beneath which Moses first encountered God in the Burning Bush. "When the Lord saw that Moses had turned aside to look, he called to him out of the Burning Bush, 'Moses! Moses!' and he answered, 'Here I am!' Then God said to him, 'Do not come near! Take off your sandals, for the place where you are standing is holy ground'" (Exodus 3:3-5). Moses knew that desert very well, every spring and cave and oasis. Suddenly the familiar became unfamiliar as he spotted something strange about a bush. He turned aside to look—and he encountered God. If we want to encounter God, we also have to turn aside and look—we have to be alert to his coming. To do this we have to curb the relentless distraction that dissipates our energies and frays the life of our society, of which the smartphone is a lively symbol. Do we know in which direction to turn, however?

Many centuries later, the prophet Elijah, fleeing for his life, also encountered God on Sinai. Climbing up above the monastery are the precipitous stairs towards the summit, just below which is a small declivity and a chapel alongside a cave associated with the prophet's experience. "The Lord said to Elijah, 'Go and stand on the mountain before the Lord.' The Lord was passing by: a great and strong wind came, rending the mountains and shattering rocks before him; but the Lord was not in the wind; and after the wind there was an earthquake; but the Lord was not in the earthquake; and after the earthquake a fire; but the Lord was not in the fire; and after the fire came a sound of gentle stillness. When Elijah heard this, he wrapped his face in his cloak and went out to stand at the entrance of the cave. A voice came to him: 'Why are you here, Elijah?'" (1 Kings 19:11-13).

The Hebrew phrase "a sound of gentle stillness" recalls how God conversed with Adam and Eve in the garden of Paradise in the cool of the evening. Human beings are designed to be able to sense the immediate reality of God, even if they cannot see him with their physical eyes. For there is an innate affinity between God and humanity, a capacity to respond with awe and love to his nearness. Do we listen for God in order to be able to listen to God? Once again, we have to turn off the relentless noise generated by our society with its intrusive social and entertainment media. Instead, we have to be still and silent in ourselves, in the hope of catching the whisper of divine love.

The Psalmist is quite direct about this: "Let be—be still, and know that I am God" (Psalm 46:10). "Stand in awe and sin not: commune with your heart upon your bed, and be silent and still" (Psalm 4:4). Notice that this is a divine command, not just an expression of wishful religious thinking. We will not come to know God unless we are still, unless we let go of all that clutters our life and thinking, just as Moses had to discard his sandals and stand vulnerable and still in the presence of God. When this happens, every place becomes holy ground, for there God is present. Whether we pray standing, sitting, kneeling, or even in bed, the goal is the same—to be silent and still in order to know the immensity of God's silent love and presence.

In the midst of tragedy and exile, the prophet in the book of Lamentations said: "It is good to hope and quietly wait for the salvation of the Lord: let them sit alone and keep silence, because the Lord has laid this upon them" (Lamentations 3:26–8). Stillness in the presence of God is not something just for our wellbeing: it is an engagement with God, and an entering into the silence of his presence. It may plunge us deeper into the world's pain and darkness, and draw us nearer to the silence of the Cross. Many human beings experience the humiliating silence of despair and defeat, of humiliation, imprisonment and degradation. Christians stand alongside them, as does Christ himself, within the silent prayer of his suffering love; for as Dietrich Bonhoeffer once said, "Christians stand by God in his hour of grieving."

The Gospels portray Jesus asleep in a boat suddenly caught up in a storm on the Sea of Galilee: "Jesus awoke and rebuked the wind, and said to the sea, 'Peace, be still!' The gale ceased, and there was a great calm" (Mark 4:39). By so doing he demonstrated his authority as the Son of God, the Messiah; he exercised his creative power as the Word of God. One of the most memorable moments in the pandemic was when Pope Francis preached on this text in Holy Week 2020, standing alone in a windswept piazza in front of St Peter's in Rome as the universal pastor of the Church. Into the vortex of human sin and suffering, Christ still speaks, "Peace, be still!" The darkness of evil cannot overwhelm his silent and suffering presence. Into the inner storms of personal human confusion and sorrow, these words bring us directly the promise of his nearness and comfort: "Peace I leave with you: my peace I give to you" (John 14:27).

Jesus teaches with simplicity and immediacy the way to encounter the peace of God's presence: "When you pray, enter your inner chamber, shut the door and pray to your Father who is in secret" (Matthew 6:6). Privacy was hard to achieve in ordinary homes at that time with everyone living in a common room: the Greek word actually means "go into the broom cupboard"! Jesus withdrew often into the countryside to pray, followed in due course by his disciples. He wished to encounter his Father in stillness and silence—and alone. His example should guide us too; for the simple question is whether we truly seek God with our whole heart. If we do, we should seek him in silence, and we shall encounter him. As we quietly knock, we may hear his knocking on the door of our heart. "Behold, I stand at the door and knock" (Revelation 3:20). What should we ask of him, and what does he ask of us? "Be still and know that I am God" (Psalm 46:10). His peace is his gift to us in Jesus Christ; and our hearts will remain restless until they find their rest in him—within the profound silence of his love.

43

The Mystery of Faith

A sermon for Eastertide

"Great is the mystery of faith: Christ has died; Christ is risen; Christ will come again." Often when we celebrate Holy Communion, we use these words as our response to the words of the consecrating prayer, by which bread and wine become for us the Body and Blood of Christ. Every time that we celebrate Holy Communion, and especially on Sundays, we celebrate the death and resurrection of Jesus. These words encapsulate its mystery.

"Great is the mystery of faith." We only ever stand on the edge of the profound mystery revealed in the Cross and resurrection of Jesus—the mystery of God's creating, redeeming and loving purpose for us and for the world. Just as we can hardly begin to fathom how the world came into being in the first place, so we can hardly come to terms with the promise with which the Bible ends: "Behold, I am making all things new" (Revelation 21:5). In Jesus, God the Creator comes as re-creator; and it is interesting to read closely the healing miracles of Jesus to discern the hidden note of re-creation evident within them.

"Christ has died." Careful reflection on the meaning of Holy Week and Good Friday should enable us to begin to come to terms with the stark impact of these words. The death of Jesus was a real death, and his suffering was appalling. Yet in the words of Paul, "God was in Christ reconciling the world unto himself" (2 Corinthians 5:19). This is because "one died for all, therefore all died" (2 Corinthians 5:14). As a result, "if anyone is in Christ there is a new creation" (2 Corinthians 5:17). When we renew the promises made at our baptism and confirmation, we affirm this profound truth, the mystery of our being "in Christ". For "all who are baptized into Jesus Christ are baptized into his death" (Romans 6:3). We accept the self-giving of God in Jesus as we accept the Body of Christ that is given for us and to us in Holy Communion.

"Christ is risen." In the Cross and resurrection of Jesus, the divine principle at the heart of the world's existence and of human history is revealed. In the words of Paul, "if we died with Christ, we believe that we shall also live with him" (Romans 6:8); or in the words of Jesus himself, "God is not the God of the dead but of the living" (Mark 12:27). Both Jesus and Paul point us to basic truths about the created world around us, which are very evident with the beautiful onset of spring. The mystery of "living through dying" is evident in a grain of seed that falls into the ground: it gives wonderful beauty and life only as a result of losing its own separate existence (John 12:24; 1 Corinthians 15:36). Likewise, a butterfly or dragonfly emerges from long formation in an unsightly chrysalis. Human birth itself is another mystery, the formation of a complete person within the womb, who must then die to that life and emerge into this life through the trauma of birth. That person can never return to the old life. By the same analogy, in the words of Jesus to Nicodemus, "Except someone is born again and from above, that person cannot see the kingdom of God" (John 3:3). Christian faith in the resurrection is central to our worship and also to our pastoral care of others, for example at funerals. It is not a blind faith, however, but a costly and exacting faith, as we allow ourselves to be embraced by the healing love of God himself as he comes to us in Jesus.

"Christ will come again." At the end of Paul's first letter to the Corinthians, there is an ancient Aramaic prayer: "*Maranatha*—Our Lord comes" (1 Corinthians 16:22). It appears in Greek at the end of Revelation: "Amen—come, Lord Jesus!" We know from an early Christian text called the *Didache* that this prayer in Aramaic was closely associated with the consecrating prayer of the Eucharist. Anything remembered in Aramaic and embedded in the Greek of the New Testament is a precious link with the earliest followers of Jesus. We may feel daunted and rightly mystified by Christian belief in the coming of Christ at the end of the age. We can take to heart personally, however, the challenge of Jesus in Revelation: "Behold, I stand at the door and knock: if anyone hears my voice and opens the door, I will come in and eat with them and they with me" (Revelation 3:20). This wonderful promise was borne out in the Easter experience of the two disciples walking back from Jerusalem to Emmaus, who invited the stranger into their home to break bread with them (Luke 24:29–32): as Jesus said, "I was a stranger and you took me in" (Matthew 25:35).

The mystery of the presence of the risen Jesus stands at the heart of the Eucharist, which has been celebrated each week since the beginning of Christianity. With its roots in Jewish observation of the Passover, its meaning is defined by the death and resurrection of Jesus. It is a celebration of his death and also of his resurrection, and of his personal presence among us, because Jesus promises that "someone who eats me will also live because of me ... for my flesh is true food and my blood is true drink ... someone who eats my flesh and drinks my blood has eternal life, and I will raise that person up at the last day" (John 6:53–9). In these words, the end of all things is rooted in that which is present here and now at the heart of our faith, our life and of human history—Jesus Christ crucified and risen.

Eternal life is therefore a reality now that points forward to an eternal existence hereafter. Whereas the foetus in the womb has no control over its destiny, the human being within the womb of this life has the crucial choice whether to accept or reject the love of God revealed in Jesus. God cannot compel human love; but in Christ he appeals to each one of us in the solemn and moving words, "This is my body that is given for you." Who would spurn such a loving gift?

This is why it is now imperative that regular celebrations of Holy Communion in our churches are restored as soon as possible after the disastrous interruption of the sacrament over the past unhappy months. With due care, there is no risk in receiving the sacrament. Undue fear has no place in Christian worship, "for perfect love casts out fear" (1 John 4:18). By receiving Holy Communion, "we know that we have passed out of death into life" (1 John 3:14). The death and resurrection of Jesus is the abolition of all fear, for "Christ has risen from the dead: by death he has trampled on death; and to those in the grave he gives life."

4 4

Sursum Corda

The story about the unknown woman with a chronic stoop, whom Jesus healed in a synagogue on the Sabbath Day, is told only in Luke's Gospel (Luke 13:10–17). Its dramatic character occurred in a situation where men and women sat separately to worship, and where rabbis never addressed or touched a woman who was not their own wife. It is one of a sequence of stories in every Gospel in which Jesus' healing on the Sabbath posed a real challenge to his religious critics, as well as asserting his authority to act in this way on behalf of God.

I never read or hear this moving story without remembering seeing it sadly in reverse in the first parish in which I was serving as a curate. There was a devout and charming lady, who worshipped regularly in our church, but whose life was weighed down by an alcoholic husband and a tearaway teenage son. One day, having just returned from holiday, I saw her in the High Street completely bent down. Her woes had clearly got on top of her and her body expressed their impact. My colleague, the rector, and I were dismayed—and felt completely powerless to help her effectively. I left the parish shortly afterwards and did not hear the end of her story.

Priests often encounter situations like this that leave them feeling deeply frustrated and sad. When friends ask me why I attach such importance to pastoral ministry in parishes, it is because I am sure that no family or individual should feel unsupported and uncared for. The priest is there to help families and individuals round the tight corners in life that come to us all. Very often the kitchen table in a home is the other altar, as people pour out their hearts to a priest, who has called by to listen to them, and to show an encouraging interest in their lives.

All Christians are called to share in this pastoral ministry by being alert to the needs of others in a kind and non-judgemental way. Indeed, any Christian is actually where a priest cannot be, in the midst of a unique web of relationships; and so in a strong parish there should always be a mature and trusting partnership between priest and laity in the care of others. The particular vocation of Anglican Christianity is to offer this help and support to anyone in a community, whether they come to church or not. This is why the parish system needs to be maintained and valued. A Gospel story like this one sets us all a fine example.

In many of the miracles of Jesus such as this one, what happened outwardly sheds light on what is needed inwardly. He went across to her as she lurked in the shadows; he spoke with her and listened to her; he embraced her and raised her up; he liberated her from a crushing burden that had distorted her life for eighteen hard and wearisome years. She lived in a religious society that taught that such illness was a punishment from God for sins committed by her, or perhaps by her parents. Part of the mission of Jesus was to break this tyranny of opinion, hence the sharp reactions from his religious critics, as well as the joy of some of his hearers.

Jesus came to liberate people from their inner burdens—of fear and guilt and sin, of trauma and hurt; just like Pilgrim in *The Pilgrim's Progress*, who at the Cross found that his burden rolled away. This is why in every service we confess our sins and seek absolution. By so doing, we express our loving and penitent solidarity with all those around us who are in a similar plight as sinners before God, from whom no secrets can be hidden. Part of a priest's work is to hear private confessions also. No-one need be trapped in their sins and unhappiness.

This woman was bowed down and unable to look up. St Bonaventure taught that this symbolizes the plight of every fallen human being, unable to look up in the direction of God, and fixated on the things of this created world as ends in themselves. Every human society, from the poorest to the richest, is prone to this. In our own society, the greatest enemy to Christianity is in fact distraction. The aim of a consumer society is always to keep people focused on the next purchase, the latest fashion. A good symbol of this is the mobile phone, to which many people give inordinate attention, at home, and out and about. A new advertisement on the London Underground says simply—"Mind the gap and not the app!"

More tragically, people can easily become bowed down by obsessions promoted by consumerism: the next car, a new home, the latest fashion; or more obviously destructively, the compulsion of alcoholism or drug abuse, of pornography, or the inordinate love of money. Finally, many everywhere are simply oppressed, bowed down by circumstances like poverty, or cruelty in family life and relationships. Sometimes whole countries can succumb to such an oppressive legacy from which they cannot escape, inflicting violence on their neighbours in a vicious cycle stretching back centuries, as is tragically apparent in the war between Russia and Ukraine.

Jesus said that "I have come that they may have life—life in all its fullness" (John 10:10). This is why we stand to hear the Gospel in church, and also for the consecrating prayer of the Eucharist. "Lift up your hearts! We lift them to the Lord. Let us give thanks to the Lord our God: it is meet and right so to do." These words are some of the earliest Christian prayers and have always prefaced the consecrating prayer. This is because we are bidden to stand in the presence of God as those who have been liberated from the downward bias and blindness of sin: no more cowering in the bushes, hiding from God and clutching fig-leaves! For "the Lord is the Spirit: and where the Spirit of the Lord is, there is liberty: so, we all with unveiled faces, reflecting as a mirror the glory of the Lord, are being transformed into the same image from glory to glory, by the Lord the Spirit" (2 Corinthians 3:17–18).

Returning to the Gospel story once again, we see that there were two other people who were stooped down, one actually and the other metaphorically. The ruler of the synagogue responded in a frustrated and institutionalized manner, protesting that such disturbance should occur in divine worship. Jesus exposed the folly of his tunnel-vision and its innate hypocrisy and cruelty in terms that were clearly not forgotten by those who witnessed it. Indeed, it is possible that this was actually a moment of liberation for some of them, perhaps even for the ruler of the synagogue himself. St Paul certainly testified to the crushing nature of the sense of obligation to the Law of God for so many at that time and the barrenness of being obsessed with its literal interpretation.

The other person who stooped down was, of course, Jesus himself, bending over to hear the whispered story of this unhappy woman, who was confined to the margins of her society. St Augustine once said that "proud people could only be saved by the humble God", and the humility of Jesus was his hidden strength because it sprang from God himself. This is one of the great themes of Luke's Gospel, culminating in Jesus, staggering and bowed down by his own Cross, and yet able to pray for his tormentors, who were lost in their own darkness, blindness and cruelty.

We too are called to stoop down willingly in humility in order to come alongside others in a kind and non-patronizing way. We are called to stoop as we receive the mystery of Holy Communion, saying to the Lord, "I am not worthy that you should come under my roof: but speak the word only and I shall be healed." We are called to stoop in our hearts as we contemplate the humility and love of God in the tiny baby of Bethlehem, born in a cave or an underground outhouse. We are also called to stoop in wonder in order to peer into the Empty Tomb, and then, like the women, to fall at the feet of our Lord in loving worship, and to hear him say to us also, "Peace be with you."

45

The Mirror of the Annunciation

> The Lord is in the midst of you, as a mighty one who will save you:
>   fear no evil.
> He will rejoice over you with great joy;
>   He will silently delight in renewing you in his love.
> He will rejoice over you with singing:
>   for exalted in the midst of you is the Holy One.
>
> *Zephaniah 3:15–17 and Isaiah 12:6*

One of the joys and privileges of being a grandparent is once again to treasure the arrival of a baby and to receive the jubilant delights of young children. Every parent has many such moments, but relentless tiredness often clouds later memory. Now the miraculous encounter comes round again as a pure gift of God. For in the tiny child may be sensed the hidden wonder of the soul; and in the exuberant affection of children may be glimpsed the generous heart of God. Jesus placed children as central in his teaching, welcoming them and saying, "of such is the Kingdom of God" (Mark 10:14). This is why children are baptized and cherished in the life of the Church.

The words of these two prophets, Zephaniah and Isaiah, capture well the overwhelming experience of love that pours forth from our hearts towards a new baby and a little child. Tenderness, joy, hope, delight, wonder—all these manifestations of the love that human beings share with God himself. In the presence of a new-born baby, you are never closer to sensing that each person is indeed made in the image and likeness of God, except perhaps at the bedside of someone who is dying. These words of the prophet echo the *Magnificat* itself—Mary's hymn of praise at the Annunciation. At Christmas, we celebrate the simple and humble human reality of the coming of Jesus into the loving embrace of Mary and Joseph and their wider families in Bethlehem and Nazareth. This is no sentimental fairy story or legend: this is the miracle of God becoming a human child in Jesus.

It is something more: it is a mirror for us of divine love, of the heart of God himself, who wishes to delight in each of his children. He wishes to dispel the fear of evil from our hearts. He alone can offer us salvation as healing and inner security—to make us know that we are truly loved by him for the unique person that we are. If we turn to him in our prayers and in our hearts, we will find him coming to us to delight in us and to renew us in his love; and to renew our love of him. As we enter more deeply through love and prayer and worship, we begin to sense the great joy of heaven over each sinner who repents, each person who returns to their heavenly Father who is patiently waiting for them. As we hear Jesus knocking on the door of our hearts and open ourselves to his hidden presence within us, so we exalt him as the true Lord of our lives, who shares his life with us and who gives himself to us, saying, "This is my body which is given to and for you."

The implications of this vision of divine love are far-reaching and profound. For each human child is of value to God and should be of value to us and to our society. Christian ethics should always have the interests of the child at the centre. If this were truly the case in our society, its values and behaviour would change. This needs also to be true in so many situations around the world of poverty and upheaval, where the wellbeing of children is at risk, and the hearts of parents are torn apart by pressures that they cannot overcome. Our hearts go out to them at Christmas time; and the impulse of our hearts should be matched by our charitable giving to those in need.

To receive the tiny fragment of bread at Holy Communion is to open our hearts to Jesus who comes among us. Its fragility reminds us of the fragility of his humanity—indeed of all humanity. How can the child in the manger end up tortured on the Cross? This grim challenge confronts us as we remember that in John's Gospel the word "exalt" means Jesus being lifted up onto the Cross, and only there revealing his divine glory—the outpouring of divine love "to put love in where love is not". If we treasure the Christ-child at Bethlehem, we have also to follow him to Calvary and to bear his Cross. The hearts of all human beings are judged by the Cross of Christ. Let us not find ourselves on the wrong side of the Cross.

God wishes us to respond to him in love. He calls us in Jesus to return to him and to place our lives at the centre of the eternal beam of his redeeming light and love, to face him and not to hide from him. He cannot force this relationship, but he waits for us throughout our lives on earth. Make this your daily prayer: "Jesus, I love you and I give myself to you." As you pray this, you are responding to his hidden words to you: "I love you too, and I give myself to you." Each time you receive Holy Communion, say to him in gratitude: "Lord Jesus Christ, I need only one thing in this world: to know myself and to love you. Give me day by day your grace and your love; for with these I am rich enough, I desire nothing more. Amen."

4 6

Why we have Faces

A reflection for the feast of the Transfiguration of our Lord

In Luke's account of the Transfiguration of Jesus on the mountain, it was "as Jesus was praying that the appearance of his face was altered and his clothing became white and dazzling" (Luke 9:29). In Matthew's account, Jesus "was transfigured before them: his face shone like the sun, and his garments became white as light" (Matthew 17:2). In Revelation, the seer John fell down at the feet of the Lord himself, whose "countenance was like the sun shining at its full strength" (Revelation 1:16). For in the light of Christ's Transfiguration, we know that "God is light, and in him is no darkness at all" (1 John 1:5). God's glory shines through the face and person of Jesus as through a lens, making his invisible reality clear and visible in human form.

The face of Jesus reveals to us the glory of God in a way to which we can relate if we truly seek his face. The face of Jesus also reveals to us our own destiny, the reason why we have faces at all. Each human face is unique because it is designed to express by worship and in love the Christ-like image and likeness of God in which each individual person is made.

It is an interesting fact that although Christians have sometimes veiled their heads, it has seldom been the custom to mask the face in Christian prayer or in public worship. There are two reasons for this. Firstly, Christian worship and prayer engages with others within the love of God, and the face is an important means of communication and fellowship. Secondly, we pray to God that our hearts may be open to him, "from whom no secrets are hidden". The downfall of humanity in the beginning was hiding from God and no longer looking him in the eye; but you cannot hide from God.

Christ came into the world to restore human beings, and to enable us to begin again to approach God as our loving and forgiving heavenly Father. In the words of the Prodigal Son, "I will return to my Father and say unto him: I have sinned against heaven and against you and I am no longer worthy to be called your son" (Luke 15:18–19). He had to return to face his father and to look him in the eye, in order to say these words sincerely.

In the words of St Paul, "We all with unveiled faces, beholding and reflecting as in a mirror the glory of the Lord, are transformed into the same image from glory to glory, as from the Spirit who is the Lord" (2 Corinthians 3:18). This is because "God, who said in the beginning that light shall shine out of darkness, has shone in our hearts to give the light of the knowledge of the glory of God in the face of Jesus Christ" (2 Corinthians 4:6). The more we look into the face of Jesus Christ the more we shall see truly ourselves in him.

"The glory of God in the face of Jesus Christ." Here is the heart of the Christian faith, the wellspring of our worship "in spirit and in truth" (John 4:24). For if it remains true that "no-one has seen God at any time", it is also true that "God the only-begotten, the Son who is intimate with the Father, he has expressed him" (John 1:18). This means that, in words of Archbishop William Temple, "God is Christ-like, and in him is nothing un-Christ-like at all."

This also means that all Christian prayer and worship is in the immediate presence of Christ. This is encapsulated in the words of the Jesus Prayer: "Lord Jesus Christ, Son of the Living God, have mercy upon me, a sinner." Christ stoops down to raise us up to stand in his presence with open faces and unashamed, to look upon him with love and trust. He wishes to restore us to a right relationship with God. As St Bonaventure put it so movingly in *The Mystical Vine*: Jesus calls to us, pleading for our love and attention, saying that "the reason I became visible was in order that you might see me and give me your love . . . I gave myself to you: will you give yourself to me?"

"Blessed are the pure in heart: for they shall see God" (Matthew 5:8). This promise of Jesus holds out to each one of us the hope and promise of seeing God "face to face", even though "now we see only in a mirror obscurely, but then face to face" (1 Corinthians 13:12). These words of Paul are corroborated by words from the first letter of John: "Beloved, we are already children of God, but it is not yet clearly revealed what we shall be. We only know that when he is revealed, we shall be like him; for we shall see him as he is" (1 John 3:2). Only by contemplating the face of Jesus Christ does a person become truly Christ-like, as his glory becomes reflected in and through our faces and our lives. This is the purpose of our prayer and worship, privately and in church, and this is why reading the Gospel each day is so important so that we come to know who Jesus truly is.

Sometimes in Christian history, this mystery of divine glory, of the Uncreated Light of God, has been glimpsed in the faces of saints: for example, Moses receiving the Law of God on Sinai; Francis receiving the stigmata; Columba praying on Iona; Catherine of Siena in the presence of the Eucharist; Seraphim of Sarov walking with a friend through a snowy Russian forest. The transfiguration of the human person is therefore a reality as well as an ultimate hope. Each person is made in the image and likeness of God; and as the image and likeness are restored in Christ, so through that unique person the glory of God may be glimpsed in a unique way. The Bible closes with this great promise: "They shall see his face, for his name will be upon their foreheads" (Revelation 22:4). To receive the Cross in Baptism is to walk in this way and to be marked in love by God as his own.

In the Old Testament, the hope of Israel was sometimes expressed in relation to God's face or countenance: "Lord, lift up the light of Thy countenance upon us" (Psalm 4:6); "Blessed are the people that can rejoice in Thee: they shall walk in the light of Thy countenance" (Psalm 89:15). Why is this so? It is because it is only if God looks at us that we can begin to look at him: "for with Thee is the well of life: and in Thy light shall we see light" (Psalm 36:9). In fact, God looks at us all the time, otherwise we could not exist: "His eyes behold and try the children of men ... for the Lord is righteous and he loveth righteousness. His countenance beholds the upright, and the upright shall behold his face" (Psalm 11:5,7). Only in Christ can we become upright again, and only in the righteousness of Christ can we come into God's presence. Let us make these words of the Psalmist our own: "My heart hath talked of Thee: seek ye my face: Thy face, Lord, will I seek. O hide not Thy face from me, nor cast Thy servant away in displeasure" (Psalm 27:8-9).

PART 7

A Cloud of Witnesses

47

The Prayer of Mary

Luke 1:26-38

"Behold, I am the handmaid of the Lord: be it unto me according to your word." Seldom can so few words have affected the lives of so many people throughout hundreds of years. These are some of the rare words from Mary herself in the Gospels, but in so many ways they are the key to being and becoming a Christian.

Behold!

"Behold, a virgin shall conceive and bear a son and shall call his name Emmanuel", which means "God is with us" (Isaiah 7:14). "Behold" signifies alertness to the nearness of God. It is as if Mary suddenly realized who was actually addressing her by means of the angel. Turning to God, she said in her youthful simplicity, "Look—here I am." Her turning to God was a response to the sense that he was approaching her first. She sensed that God valued her as a person made in his image and likeness. It was as if he was calling her by name—"Mary". Our response to God is always because he has come to us first. Do we hear his call? Will we obey?

I am

We only exist at all because God beholds us, as he holds us within the beam of his creating love. Which way will we face? If we turn to him, we may stand in his light and within it we will see light. Our Christian path is thus a constant turning to him, a constant seeking of the focal point of his redeeming love, so that we might stand there facing him in love alone. If we turn aside from him, however, we enter the shadows of distraction. If we turn our backs on him completely, we will wander away from him into darkness; and in the end, darkness means death, because our life needs God's light in order to survive and to thrive. This is why the key question of Baptism and Confirmation is, "Do you turn to Christ?"

The handmaid

The humility of God called forth the humility of Mary. His coming to be among human beings as a tiny baby within her womb was an astonishing act of self-emptying and self-giving. God wishes us to relate to him with the sensitive and overflowing love that we feel towards a tiny child. This is why the interests of children are central to Christian faith and ethics: children are God's sign to us of the nature of his love. Mary recognized her obligation to God, something inculcated within her by her devout Jewish faith. Her humility and love left its mark on her child, Jesus, who came not to be served but to serve. Although the soul is beyond gender, it is often described as feminine, called to become the Bride of Christ. We are all therefore called to be handmaids and servants of the Lord.

Of the Lord

Mary's response reveals the length and breadth, the height and depth of what it means to encounter and submit to the Lordship of God as he comes to us in Jesus, her son. St John of the Cross wrote in a poem: "With the Divine Word, the Virgin made pregnant comes walking down the road to you, if you will grant her room in your heart." The nature of the Lordship of Christ is revealed in the manner of his coming, as Jesus is held in the embrace of his holy mother, Mary. As St Augustine once said, "Proud man can only be saved by the humble God." The full measure of God the Trinity comes to a focus in Jesus, as the Father and the Holy Spirit bring forth the Incarnation of the Son of God, who is also the son of Mary.

Be it unto me

With these words came Mary's assent, her "Amen". She could have said, "No". In fact, she said, "Yes", as God placed himself in the person of his Son into her hands—within her womb as in a sanctuary: "Rejoice, enclosure of the uncontained God: rejoice, doorway of a solemn mystery!"—words from the Orthodox Akathist Hymn. Throughout the Gospel, Mary faced hard choices as she fulfilled the commitment of these words. She could not possess her son at the wedding: but she told his disciples, "Whatever he says to you, do it" (John 2:5). She had to hear hard words from Jesus, which seemed to repudiate her own family when he said, "Who is my mother and my brethren?" Looking around on those sitting at his feet, he said, "Behold, my mother and my brethren! For whoever does the will of God, that person is my brother, and sister, and mother" (Mark 3:33–5). Thus, the vocation of Mary was vindicated by Jesus in a hard way; but in the process it becomes our vocation also: to do the will of God, and so to become the true and loving family of Christ. Mary leads the way for us into this holy human family, on earth and in heaven.

According to thy word

One of the governing words in the Gospel is the little word "as". "Love one another as I have loved you" (John 13:34; 15:12); "As the Father has loved me, I also have loved you" (John 15:9); "As the Father has sent me, so I send you" (John 20:21). Here is the heart of Christianity: to live within the love of God himself, Father, Son and Holy Spirit. But this saving word of divine love comes to us often at great cost, as Mary discovered when she took her tiny first-born son into the Temple. The devout old man, Simeon, took up the child and spoke the wonderful words of the *Nunc Dimittis*. Then he blessed the parents; but he said to Mary, "Behold, this child is set for the falling and rising up of many in Israel, as a sign to be spoken against. Indeed, a sword will pierce through your own soul, so that the thoughts of many hearts may be revealed" (Luke 2:34–5). These terrible words found their grim fulfilment as Mary witnessed the crucifixion of her son. "When Jesus saw his mother and the disciple whom he loved standing by, he said to his mother, 'Woman, behold your son!' Then he said to the disciple, 'Behold your mother!' and he took her immediately into his own family" (John 19:26–7). This charge pierces our hearts too: will we welcome this suffering mother and her son into our hearts and lives?

Theotokos

St Hugh, Bishop of Lincoln, who died in 1200, was the last great monk-bishop of the English Church. He was a person of deep and loveable sanctity, but also formidable capacity as a leader of the Church. He was the inspiration behind the beautiful design and building of Lincoln Cathedral, while remaining a simple Carthusian monk. He always showed marked respect towards women, saying that "God well deserves to be loved by women, for he did not shun being born of a woman. Marvellous and precious was the privilege he thus gave to all women: for it was not granted to a man to be, or to be called, 'father of God'; but it was given to a woman to bear God." This is why Mary is acclaimed and loved as the *Theotokos*, the bearer of God the Word, and therefore truly the "Mother of God". She is also Mother of the Church and of the saints, and of all true Christians who cherish and obey Jesus her son and who pray, "Most Holy Mother of God, save us by your prayers." Each day, and particularly as we come to receive Holy Communion, let us make her prayer our own: "Behold, I am the servant of the Lord: may it be unto me according to your word. Amen."

4 8

Mary—Mother and Martyr

A sermon for Mothering Sunday

There is a small parish church, set in a quiet courtyard in Nicosia in Cyprus and hard by the green line of frozen conflict that still divides that city. It is beautifully maintained and prayed in, and full of a rich range of very old icons, some of them rescued from the area of Turkish occupation close by. One icon is of the holy Mother of the Lord: the face is about the size of a child's face. Looking closely at it, several layers of paint and restoration can be glimpsed, reaching down in places to the level of the original image. Suddenly, the original eye of the Virgin seemed to become alive, with a penetrating gaze of sorrow and sensitivity that pierced the soul. Hundreds of years of worship and suffering overlay and encased her silent witness and presence.

No-one can read the story of the crucifixion of Jesus in John's Gospel (John 19:25–7) without being moved by the exchange between Jesus and his mother, who was witnessing his torture and death. He entrusted her to the care of his closest disciple and friend with the words, "Woman, behold thy son!" and "Behold thy mother!" These words have inspired some of the greatest Christian art and poetry, notably the medieval hymn *Stabat Mater*. It is nonetheless shocking that any mother should have to witness the brutal murder of her own son. It is to this terrible truth that the ancient icon in Nicosia also bore witness. Mary the Mother is also Mary the Martyr—in Latin the words *Mater* and *Martyr* sound very close indeed. So, any veneration of Mary the Mother of the Lord has to be rooted in this grim reality, this indictment of human cruelty in every age. It is a tragic fact that on this Mothering Sunday, such cruelty is still being perpetrated across the world, as human rights are abused, and Christians are persecuted.

Mary knew from the beginning that it would end in tears. Confronted by the old man, Simeon, in the Temple, the young parents of the child Jesus were haunted by the strange prediction that he made to Mary: "Behold, this child is set for the falling and rising up of many in Israel, and as a sign that will be spoken against. Indeed, a sword will pierce through your own soul, so that the thoughts of many hearts may be revealed" (Luke 2:34–5). It is her authority that lies behind the opening chapters of Luke's Gospel, for Mary "kept all these things, pondering them in her heart" (Luke 2:19,51). Matthew's Gospel records the flight of the Holy Family into Egypt, leaving behind them a dreadful massacre of children in and around Bethlehem. "A voice was heard in Ramah, weeping and great mourning: Rachel weeping for her children, who could not be comforted because they were destroyed" (Matthew 2:18, citing Jeremiah 31:15). The commemoration of the Holy Innocents shortly after Christmas itself is an annual reminder that such events continue today, casting the shadow of the Cross over the birth of Jesus himself.

When Mary said to the angel, "Behold, I am the servant of the Lord: may it be unto me according to your word" (Luke 1:38), could she have imagined at that moment how her life would unfold? Under pressure from her extended family, she and they accosted Jesus one day early in his teaching ministry. But he asked, "Who is my mother and my brethren?" In repudiating the claims of kinship in such a close-knit society, Jesus nonetheless affirmed the heart of his mother's vocation, and his own true relationship with her, when he said, "whoever does the will of God is truly my brother and sister and my mother" (Mark 3:31–5). A similar note of confrontation and affirmation is encountered early in John's Gospel at the wedding feast in Cana. The words of Jesus remembered there only make sense in the light of the Cross to which he made a cryptic allusion, saying to his mother, "My hour has not yet come." Mary's response, however, was one of obedience and trust: "Whatever he says to you, do it" (John 2:4–5). With these words she addresses all of us who would truly follow and cherish her son Jesus.

Mary's role in nurturing the life of the earliest Church passes into later Christian tradition. The last explicit mention of her in the New

Testament is in the Acts of the Apostles, when she joined the twelve disciples in prayer in Jerusalem after the ascension of Jesus and before the descent of the Holy Spirit on the day of Pentecost (Acts 1:14). Hints of her significance occur elsewhere in the earliest strata of Christian witness, however. For example, in these words of Paul: "God chose the foolish things of the world, to put to shame the wise; and God chose the weak things of the world to put to shame the strong; and base things that are despised, even things that count for nothing, to bring to nothing things that are" (1 Corinthians 1:27–8). This conviction is very close to the spirit of the *Magnificat* itself. In the society in which Mary lived, the testimony of a teenage mother counted for very little, especially if people thought that she had conceived her child out of marriage; Mary and Jesus had to live under this stigma.

Finally in Revelation, there is the mysterious figure of a pregnant woman about to be delivered, with a dragon ready at hand to consume her baby: "She was crying out in the travail of labour and in the pain of being delivered." Her child was caught up to the throne of God while she herself was shielded in a hidden place in the wilderness (Revelation 12:1–6). What might this mean? Perhaps these words of St Ignatius of Antioch, written shortly afterwards, shed some light on this mystery. "The virginity of Mary and her giving birth were hidden from the ruler of this age, as indeed was the death of the Lord—three mysteries to be loudly proclaimed now, yet which were accomplished in the silence of God ... when God appeared in human form to bring the newness of eternal life" (*Letter to the Ephesians* 19).

The figure of Mary the Mother and Martyr of the Lord should never be sentimentalized, idolized or venerated in such a way as to obscure her humble humanity and the cost of her witness. In the words of St Bonaventure: "The glorious Virgin and our Lady Holy Mary was not at a distance from Jesus when he died.... She was in travail and sorrow during the passion with the Christ, whom she had brought forth in the nativity with such joy." *Stabat Mater* is a beautiful Latin hymn, attributed most probably to the Franciscan poet Jacopone da Todi, who died in 1306:

The Mother stood there full of grief by the Cross, weeping bitterly,
For her son was hanging there.
Her soul, groaning within and lamenting,
    was racked with sorrow and sadness,
Pierced through by a sword.

49

The Making of Saints

A sermon for All Saints Day

One of the saddest things to see in an English medieval church is the way in which images of saints were scrubbed off screens and pulpits during the Reformation. The Lady Chapel of Ely Cathedral is a spectacular example of such iconoclastic desecration, with the heads knocked off every single figure in the remarkable carved frieze that runs around the inside of that lovely place. Reversing the marginalization of saints has been underway in the Church of England for over a century, and there is now more open recognition of their spiritual significance than at any time since the Reformation. The process has been greatly assisted by the diligent recovery of their history, and the careful publication of many writings of saints from across the whole Christian Church. Saints are no longer legendary figures; and their recovery has deep ecumenical significance as saints are still being declared in the Catholic and Orthodox churches. What does it mean to become a saint?

"A saint is someone who makes God real." This definition by Archbishop Michael Ramsey is a good place to start, as the first hallmark of a saint is someone with a heightened sense of God's presence and reality, who responds to the demand that his call to us in Jesus makes upon our lives—"Follow Me!" If a person orientates their life in the direction of God, he or she can become a mirror of divine reality to others. If a person submits their will freely and lovingly to the following of Christ, he or she can become like Christ in a distinctive and unique way. If such a person finds their life caught up in, and transformed by, the power of the Holy Spirit, he or she can kindle the fire of God's love in the hearts of other people. Someone once said to St Anthony in the desert of Egypt that "to see you, Father, is sufficient".

But if our lives are so distracted by material and transient preoccupations, we will not be able to sense the reality of God, any more than a person always wandering around in a shopping mall will be able to see the stars in the night sky. Are we really so busy that we cannot give priority to our prayers? Does watching television and films induce mental passivity and superficiality that is inimical to serious thought? How do we order our use of time when we are not actually at work? Do we want to spend time with God? How regularly do we read the Bible? Have you ever read the life or writings of a saint? How seriously do you prepare for Holy Communion each week? How much do you value your soul and its eternal destiny?

All Christians are called to holiness. What does this mean? It means spending time with God in prayer and worship. A saint is a person who has learnt to give this absolute priority in their daily lives, giving prime time to God in prayer, and sometimes constructing their whole day around a life of prayer. In some monasteries, prayers at night can last for several hours: monks and nuns can be in church for eight hours a day. Their vocation to a life of prayer poses a serious challenge to us all in the West, especially as monastic life has seen a marked revival on Mount Athos, in Egypt, in some parts of Eastern Europe, and in Russia.

A saint is also someone who takes the Bible seriously, reading it closely and prayerfully. In the early and medieval Church, people actually learnt Scripture by heart, beginning with the psalms. A saint will often look back to the life and teaching of an earlier saint, taking their example and writings to heart as a foundation for life. He or she will never feel alone in their own vocation, but rather draw on the deep spiritual riches and traditions of the Christian Church. A saint is therefore someone who allows the Holy Spirit to lead them into all truth, which means a life-long education, formation and commitment. Their spiritual life points beyond itself to the eternal life and love of God.

As in a good marriage or a strong friendship, time spent with another person alters someone, hopefully for the better. This is certainly so with God. A saint is someone who becomes like God by simply being in his presence, someone in whom the love and character of Jesus may be glimpsed. What is fascinating about saints' lives is the way in which they record this process in so many varied historical and social situations. Each saint is a unique person in a particular context: they are never religious clones and certainly never boring people! No saint claims to be perfect, however, nor did their friends and disciples consider them in that light. Instead, they saw in the saint's life the pattern of the Gospel repeated and made real: the compassion of Jesus, the clarity of his teaching, and his example. They also often witnessed the pain of following Christ so closely, as many saints' lives were marked by illness and suffering, by hostility and persecution. They demonstrated the force of the teaching of Jesus in the Sermon on the Mount about the narrow gate and the afflicted way that leads to eternal life. Through their lives, healing often flowed into the lives of others, during their lifetime and after their death. Their burial places often became shrines—places where holiness could be sensed, and signs of the hope of the resurrection.

The sense of God, being with God, becoming like God—this is the pattern of sanctity to which we are each called. The challenge of All Saints-tide is to become what we are called to be in Christ. As St Augustine once said, "Christians see set before them on the altar that which they are called to become." Consider the silver chalice of the Eucharist: something precious, dedicated for a unique task; something that has to be utterly clean and prepared, standing stable on the altar and entirely open to heaven, looking upwards and waiting for the descent of the Holy Spirit upon the gifts of bread and wine. Some saints have actually witnessed the fire of the Spirit descend on the consecrated gifts, fire that can touch our lips and make us clean and holy. As we approach Holy Communion, we should make these words of Psalm 63 our own:

> O God, thou art my God: early, eagerly, and earnestly will I seek Thee:
> My soul thirsts for Thee, my flesh longs for Thee,
> In a dry and weary land where there is no water.
> I look upon Thee in the sanctuary, to see Thy power and glory.
> For Thy lovingkindness is better than life itself:
> > my lips will praise Thee.

…

50

St Cuthbert

20 March and 4 September

Durham Cathedral was magnificently built shortly after the Norman Conquest as a fitting shrine to St Cuthbert, whose remains lie buried behind the high altar. In the treasury of the cathedral is an amazing array of items found in his coffin in the nineteenth century: a pectoral cross of gold and garnets; a small portable altar framed in embossed silver; silk wrappings from Byzantium from the eighth century; and fine embroidered stoles from early tenth-century Wessex. Even the original wooden casket remains, carved with outlines of saints and apostles, in which his body was enshrined soon after his death. Why was Cuthbert so highly regarded during the Anglo-Saxon centuries and throughout the Middle Ages?

Cuthbert was born around 635, the time that the Irish monk Aidan came from Iona to Northumbria by invitation of King Oswald, who had become a Christian on Iona while in exile. St Aidan founded a monastery on the tidal island of Lindisfarne, in sight of the royal fortress of Bamburgh, and this became the base for extensive missionary work by Irish monks, and later their English converts, across the north of England, the Midlands, and into East Anglia. Meanwhile, Christianity was taking root in Kent and southern England as a result of the mission of St Augustine, who arrived from Rome in 597. In time, these two strands of mission met and mingled, and after some difficulties were reconciled at the Synod of Whitby. Cuthbert, like Bede, grew up as the beneficiary of both traditions, and when Aidan died in 651, he had a vision of Aidan's soul departing to heaven, which prompted his own vocation to become a monk at the small monastery of Melrose in the Borders. Ten years later, in 661, Cuthbert, aged around 26, became prior of the monastery of Melrose, using it as a base for extensive missionary and pastoral outreach among remote and poverty-stricken villages in the surrounding hills. Around 665, he moved to become prior of the monastery of Lindisfarne.

His heart's desire, however, was the life of a hermit, which he pursued as best he could on a tiny tidal island alongside Lindisfarne, where he would retreat for the whole of Lent. In 676, he resigned as prior and moved to the Inner Farne island, which lies off the coast just south of Lindisfarne itself. He had expressed to an older friend many years earlier his dread of high office, but in 685 he was persuaded to become Bishop of Hexham by King Ecgfrith and Archbishop Theodore of Canterbury. In fact, by mutual arrangement with his friend Eata, Cuthbert swapped the post for Bishop of Lindisfarne, where he had the practical support of his own monastic community. He was an active bishop, preaching and healing as he travelled around, and warmly remembered for his kindness and spiritual example. But Cuthbert suffered from TB and, as his end approached, he withdrew again to his hermitage on the Inner Farne, where, cut off for several days by a fierce storm, his friends found him dying. Cuthbert died there on 20 March 687, aged around 50, and his body was taken back to Lindisfarne for burial.

In 698, Cuthbert's body was exhumed and found to be incorrupt. It was translated into church and placed in a carved oak casket as a focus of veneration. Many healings took place there and Lindisfarne became an important place of pilgrimage until the Vikings attacked and pillaged the place in 793. The monastic community hung on, but in 875 the monks were forced to flee further Viking attacks and become a wandering group, carrying with them the body of Cuthbert and its treasures, sometimes hiding in caves in the hills and in other places until they finally came to rest on the peninsula of Durham in 995, where the first Anglo-Saxon church was built to house Cuthbert's remains. In 1104, the body was again examined and found to be still incorrupt, and so it remained until the Reformation. Durham Cathedral remained an important and wealthy focus of pilgrimage and influence in the north of England. For Anglo-Saxon Christians, the fact that Cuthbert's body remained incorrupt was an important sign of his sanctity and its spiritual potency. It signified that he had become in his lifetime so steeped in the Holy Spirit that his mortal remains became a sign of the reality of the resurrection. St Etheldreda of Ely, who founded the monastery there in 673 and who died in 679, was also found to be incorrupt seventeen years later in 695. They were the first two Anglo-Saxon saints, and they were not the last.

Cuthbert's spiritual significance was summed up in a short but intimate *Life* composed by an anonymous Irish monk of Lindisfarne, written soon after the translation of his body and before 705. This was complemented by a poetic version by Bede based on the first anonymous *Life*, which he followed some years later with a more elaborate and theological *Life of Cuthbert*. In this work, Bede sought to interpret events in the life and ministry of Cuthbert in the light of the Gospels, taking as his example earlier lives of Christian saints. In his later *History*, Bede added further details of Cuthbert's story, including subsequent miracles associated with his tomb. During Bede's lifetime the cult of Cuthbert became well established and his writings made it widely known.

Two wonderful books remain that are closely associated with the cult of St Cuthbert. The first is the Lindisfarne Gospels, beautifully illuminated and containing a later interlinear translation of the Latin text into Anglo-Saxon. The other is a small copy of St John's Gospel that was actually found in Cuthbert's coffin in 1104. It is the earliest bound book to remain in Europe, and its Latin text is immaculately presented. Both books now reside in the British Library in London. The splendour of these books alongside the remarkable writings of Bede demonstrate how swiftly Christians became enculturated in Anglo-Saxon life, enabling the expression of their faith through literature and art. All this happened within a century of Augustine's mission to England, and in less than a century after Aidan's foundation of the monastery on Lindisfarne.

For Bede and his contemporaries, the emergence of saints like Cuthbert and Etheldreda demonstrated the active work of God the Holy Spirit in their midst, vindicating Christian evangelism rooted in prayer, example and education, and led by monks as missionaries. The memory of Cuthbert also spread wherever Anglo-Saxon missionaries worked on the Continent. For example, he is commemorated early in the eighth century in the personal calendar of St Willibrord, one of the first of the Anglo-Saxon missionaries to Germany and the Low Countries. It is very appropriate that Bede is buried at the western end of Durham Cathedral, under these words from his commentary on the book of Revelation, which proved to be true in the lives of Cuthbert and Etheldreda: "Christ is the Morning Star who, when the night of this world is past, brings to his saints the promised Light of Life, and opens to them eternal Day."

5 1

Belief without Sight

*Remembering St Alphege, St Anselm and
Archbishop Michael Ramsey in Eastertide*

Jesus said to Thomas, "Blessed are those who have not seen but yet believe" (John 20:29). In the first generation of Christianity, believing in the risen Christ without having actually seen him was a challenge, as is evident in these words of St Peter: "Having not seen him you love him, in whom you rejoice greatly with unspeakable joy and full of glory; though you see him not, yet you believe in him" (1 Peter 1:8). How is belief in the risen Jesus transmitted across the Christian generations, even to our own time? Primarily through the inspired pages of the Gospels, which contain the varied memories and witness of the closest friends of Jesus. Also in the Eucharist, celebrated each week in commemoration of the resurrection, in which Christ is present in ways that can sometimes be strongly sensed, even as he promised: "When two or three are gathered together in my Name, there am I in the midst" (Matthew 18:20). One of the earliest Christian prayers in the New Testament is the little phrase in Aramaic—*Maranatha*—"Come, Lord!" (1 Corinthians 16:22). Christ also comes to people personally, often in hidden ways, but sometimes more openly. In the book of Revelation, he says: "Behold, I stand at the door and knock: if anyone hears my voice and opens the door, I will come in and eat with him, and he with me" (Revelation 3:20).

Word, sacrament and private prayer lie at the heart of Christian belief and worship; and these are united and embodied in the active witness of those called to lead the Church spiritually and to interpret the Gospel afresh to each generation. One meaning of the phrase "apostolic succession" is precisely the way in which, like mirrors or repeater stations, the message of the Gospel is flashed from heart to heart and mind to mind across the Christian centuries. It is not customary to commemorate saints formally in Easter week, as the subtle light of their spiritual witness like stars is engulfed in the greater light of the resurrection of Jesus, the Sun of Righteousness. But this year, three notable Archbishops of Canterbury appear in Easter week, and they provide a good example of this apostolic transmission of living faith in the resurrection of Christ.

St Alphege lived in the second part of the tenth century. He was a friend and protégé of St Dunstan and St Ethelwold, who led the revival of Benedictine monastic life in England at that time. Alphege lived as a monk and hermit at Deerhurst and then somewhere in Somerset, before being made Abbot of Bath by Dunstan, who was then Archbishop of Canterbury. When Ethelwold died as Bishop of Winchester in 984, Alphege succeeded him. In 1005, he became Archbishop of Canterbury; but in 1011 he was captured by the Vikings when they besieged Canterbury. They held him hostage over the winter, expecting his people in the diocese to ransom him for the vast sum of £3,000. Alphege forbade his church to pay this ransom, knowing the poverty of his people. At a drunken feast in Greenwich, his captors pelted him to death with ox bones in their frustration. In 1023, his body was moved from St Paul's Cathedral in London back to Canterbury Cathedral, where it was interred to the north side of the high altar, opposite the burial place of Dunstan and commemorated each year on 19 April.

The new Norman Archbishop of Canterbury, Lanfranc, appointed in 1070, questioned the validity of the cult of some earlier English saints, especially those closely associated with the old regime that the Normans had overthrown by their Conquest in 1066. He turned to Anselm, his younger friend and Abbot of Bec in Normandy, for advice. Anselm's verdict was that Alphege had died like John the Baptist for the sake of justice to protect his people, and he would certainly have died willingly for his faith in Christ. In 1105, the body of Alphege was discovered to be incorrupt, and the memory of his martyrdom sustained Thomas Becket as Archbishop of Canterbury in his final crisis with King Henry II in 1170.

Anselm's wisdom served the English Church well, safeguarding the living tradition of Christian faith and worship that had developed during the long Anglo-Saxon centuries. He was an Italian from Aosta, born in 1033, who travelled north to the monastery of Bec, which was then under the intellectual leadership of Lanfranc. In 1078, he became its abbot, and after Lanfranc's death in 1089, the monks of Canterbury insisted that Anselm become their abbot as Archbishop of Canterbury. With great reluctance, Anselm accepted the invitation after King William Rufus had kept the see vacant for four years in order to milk its revenues and because he feared Anselm. He fell out with Rufus and went into exile in 1097, and things did not improve, except in personal terms, with the accession of Henry I in 1100. After a second period in exile, Anselm finally returned to England as archbishop in 1106 and died aged 76 in 1109. By 1165, with the encouragement of Thomas Becket, he was commemorated as a saint at Canterbury Cathedral on 21 April each year.

In 1720, Anselm was declared a Doctor of the Catholic Church. His life and teaching were well documented by his own writings, and also by the remarkable and readable biography written of him by his English chaplain, Eadmer. Anselm's gifts as a spiritual and intellectual teacher were second to none, and some impression of his influence upon his younger monastic pupils may be seen in his many letters. He wrote prayers that proved to be so popular and useful that they were copied and emulated for the next couple of hundred years. They are moving in their humility and directness, uniting the mind and the heart in a simple but profound manner. Anselm is remembered too as the most outstanding theologian of the Western church between Augustine and Aquinas and Bonaventure. The story is told of how, during his monastic prayers at night, he intuited that if God is that being greater than anything that exists, and because reality is always greater than any idea about it, God must exist; and the human mind, made in the divine image, is capable of perceiving this in a way that cannot be set aside once its truth is accurately grasped. This was later called the ontological argument for the existence of God.

Many centuries later, in our own times, another Archbishop of Canterbury found inspiration and strength from the memory of Anselm. Indeed, Anselm is a key to the inner spiritual life and significance of Michael Ramsey, who died in 1988 on 23 April. He told an amusing story, as his own time as archbishop was drawing to a close in 1974, about a dream he had in which he was in heaven at a party with his predecessors: "At the end a little man came up whom I immediately recognized as Anselm. When we met, we embraced each other because here I felt was a man who was primarily a don, who tried to say his prayers and who cared nothing for the pomp and glory of his position." In 1966, Michael Ramsey shared his love of Anselm with Pope Paul VI in Rome; and in 1967 he went to visit the monastery of Bec in Normandy, a place to which he returned in his retirement in 1979. He nurtured and encouraged the close ecumenical links that now exist between Bec and Canterbury Cathedral, where Anselm lies buried in a beautiful Romanesque chapel.

Michael Ramsey's verdict on the significance of Anselm is significant: "One great theme was constantly in his mind, the consistency of Christian doctrine with human reason, being governed by the principle of faith seeking understanding—*fides quaerens intellectum*." He respected Anselm's independence of mind, and his faithfulness to the Bible as the wellspring of the language of prayer. Anselm's gift for friendship, which inspired his whole approach as a teacher, also attracted Michael Ramsey. "We think of Anselm as a monk, priest and pastor. Love towards God and humility in God's presence was the root of his tenderness, sympathy, and gentleness towards those in his spiritual care." This was true of Michael Ramsey himself. Anselm could make God real to others, and this still comes across in his writings and letters, as well as in Eadmer's *Life* of him. Michael Ramsey commended and took to heart the words with which Anselm began his most famous writing, the *Proslogion*: "Come, now, little man, put aside your business for a while: take some leisure for God, and rest awhile in him."

Thus, the reality and nature of God, revealed in the resurrection of Christ, beamed across a thousand years to occupants of the same see of Canterbury, who were called to serve the Church in England. The message of the risen Christ came to them, as it does also to us: "Be still and know that I am God ... Fear not: for I am the First and the Last, the Living One, who was dead but, behold, I am alive for evermore" (Psalm 46:10; Revelation 1:17–18).

5 2

St Dunstan

19 May

Ascension Day fell on 17 May in 988 and St Dunstan preached for the last time in Canterbury Cathedral as archbishop. In fact, he preached three times at the Eucharist, and all those present "gazed on him as if he were an angel of God". Forewarned in a dream that his end was nigh, he retired to his bed and remained there, "his bald head gleaming with light". On the morning of Saturday 19 May, which is now his feast day, he received Holy Communion for the last time and bade farewell to his clergy and monks. He then began to sing words from Psalm 111: "The merciful and gracious Lord hath so done his marvellous works that they ought to be had in remembrance: He hath given meat unto them that fear him." With these words he commended his soul to God and died. He was buried in the place he had prepared within the cathedral, on the right facing the high altar, where he taught his people while living among them as their bishop.

Why should we remember Dunstan, who died over a thousand years ago? It is no exaggeration to assert that had the Norman Conquest of 1066 not occurred, Dunstan would have been remembered as one of the patron saints of England. His prominence at Canterbury Cathedral was later overshadowed by the sensational murder of Archbishop Thomas Becket in 1170 and the popular cult that grew up there as a result. The destruction of the monasteries at the Reformation is another reason why Dunstan's significance was obscured, for he was a great founder of Benedictine monasteries in the tenth century.

Dunstan was born around the year 909 and was educated at the ancient church of Glastonbury where he grew up. The first *Life of*

Dunstan records many of Dunstan's own memories of his early life there. He joined the court of King Athelstan, which was often at Cheddar; but Dunstan was not popular because of his intellectual and musical interests. His kinsman, the Bishop of Winchester, finally persuaded him to take seriously monastic life, which was being restored on the Continent at the time, following the *Rule of St Benedict*. In 942, Dunstan was appointed to reform the church of Glastonbury with a view to creating the first Benedictine monastery in England. His friend, St Ethelwold, later Bishop of Winchester, created a second one at Abingdon shortly afterwards. Some manuscripts and works of art still remain that contain evidence of Dunstan's own diligence as a scholar, musician and artist. Many of those he trained as monks there went on to become archbishops of Canterbury and bishops of the English Church for nearly a hundred years.

In 955, political upheaval caused Dunstan to flee for his life into exile in Flanders before returning as Bishop of Worcester and briefly also of London. In 960, he was made Archbishop of Canterbury by the new king, Edgar, who had been his pupil. Dunstan served as archbishop for twenty-eight years and as such had a key influence on many aspects of political life. During his time laws were drawn up that safeguarded the interests of the Danish and British populations that were now under the rule of the king of Wessex, who had become king of all England. Coinage was standardized, as were weights and measures, with stiff penalties for fraud.

The most notable monument to this important period in English history is the coronation rite. It has its roots in earlier practice in England and on the Continent, but in its present form it was largely shaped by Dunstan. It is striking that he made the coronation conditional upon the king swearing first to respect the liberty and integrity of the Church, to act consistently against theft and violence, and to rule with justice and mercy. This principle of accountability remains at the heart of the coronation rite today, as well as at the heart of English law and political process. Dunstan believed that a Christian ruler was called to be the shepherd and servant of God's people, to whom he was answerable.

The other important document remaining from Dunstan's time is the *Regularis Concordia*, which was drawn up at a synod in Winchester in 973 to regulate how monasteries were to function across England. Dunstan, Ethelwold and St Oswald, Bishop of Worcester and later Archbishop of York, were responsible for promoting the widespread foundation or refoundation of monasteries for both men and women, many of which lasted until the Reformation. At the heart of the *Regularis Concordia* is the *Rule of St Benedict*. But it also gathered together various practices from reformed monasticism on the Continent, with which Dunstan and his friends were in regular contact. It also accommodated popular English devotion and practices, notably the ringing of bells and local processions to church.

Dunstan and his contemporaries were deeply influenced by the memory of the earlier period of Anglo-Saxon church history, before the Viking assaults, as recorded by Bede in his *History*. Part of this story concerned Christian mission, and it is interesting that Dunstan promoted missionary work in Scandinavia, to which monks and bishops went from England, some of them of Danish descent. It is also striking that, so soon after the Viking invasions, there should be in the tenth century archbishops of Canterbury and York, Oda and Oskytel, who were both of Danish descent. This was a direct result of the policies of King Alfred the Great and his successors.

Some lovely manuscripts remain from this period but very little architecture or art, as all the major monastic churches and cathedrals in England were deliberately rebuilt by the Normans. Dunstan's example and initiative as an educator was very important, however, in restoring Latin learning, and also in promoting English as a means of education and expression of piety. As a result, the English Church remained bilingual before, during and long after the Norman Conquest. The roots of English medieval liturgy and prayer, that later found expression in the *Book of Common Prayer*, lie in the time of Dunstan and his colleagues.

There is a famous picture attributed directly to Dunstan while he was Abbot of Glastonbury. It portrays Christ as the Wisdom of God, standing on a hill, perhaps the Tor at Glastonbury, and holding a rod as ruler, along which are inscribed words from Psalm 45: "The rod of thy kingdom is the rod of righteousness." Christ holds an open tablet, or book, with words from another psalm that St Benedict used at the beginning of his *Rule*: "Come, my children, and listen to me; and I will teach you the fear of the Lord" (Psalm 34:11). At the feet of Christ kneels Dunstan as a monk. Above his head is a prayer that he wrote in his own handwriting:

"I, Dunstan, beg the merciful Christ to protect me, lest the storms of the underworld swallow me up!"

Dunstan's tomb in Canterbury Cathedral became a place of healing for many people, as recounted by the monks who wrote his subsequent *Lives*. It was also a place of hope, as England again faced successive Viking attacks and plundering, which finally led to the country falling under the rule of the Danish king Cnut. The memory of Dunstan also inspired prayers and music that remained in use in the English Church for many centuries. Dunstan is now commemorated in many Anglican and Catholic churches and schools named after him in this country and across the world.

5 3

Light from the Isles

Remembering St Columba and St Boniface

Sitting under the shade of a great tree last week with our latest grandchild, looking at Binham Priory church in north Norfolk, provided a graphic symbol of the Church of England: an active and lovely parish church attached to a wrecked monastery. Whatever the gains and losses of the Reformation, one of the ugliest reminders of its impact are ruined monasteries and desecrated images in churches. Norfolk bore the brunt of repeated iconoclasm under Henry VIII and later at the hands of the Puritans. Yet inside Binham church there is a further paradoxical symbol: fragments of the old rood screen remain, where texts from the Bible were painted over images of saints; but now, here and there, the faces of saints still peep through!

It is an interesting and encouraging fact that, over the last 40 years, some sense of the Christian past has been formally reaffirmed in our Church, and there are more saints now commemorated in the Anglican calendar than at any time since the Reformation. Why is it important to recall the saints, and especially those who created our church so long ago? Just as it is sad if an old person loses their memory, so it is tragic if a national Church community ages itself prematurely by forgetting its own past. Last week, we remembered two highly significant saints who were of fundamental importance to how Christianity came to England and then went from England to parts of the Continent.

First, St Columba of Iona, whose feast day falls on 9 June and who died in 597, the very year in which St Augustine came to Kent from Rome at the behest of Pope Gregory the Great. We know a great deal about Columba from two sources: a lovely body of poetry that was composed at Iona after his death and in his memory; and a first-class *Life* of the saint that was written by one of his successors as Abbot of Iona, called Adomnan, who was also a contemporary of Bede.

Columba was an Irish prince who fled political entanglements and was granted the island of Iona off western Scotland on which to found a monastery. There is a modern Christian community there today. From Iona, missionaries spread the Christian faith north across Scotland to the land of the Picts. Columba was quite capable of standing up to the local warlords, challenging their cruelty and the harsh superstitions of their pagan religion. He was also a great pastor, able to reconcile families and enemies, a champion of the poor. Iona became an important centre of scholarship, generating books in Latin and Irish that reveal a wealth of contact with the churches of the Mediterranean. The most notable thing about Columba was his sanctity; and Adomnan's *Life* portrays a deep spiritual life that was marked by visions of angels and, at times, Columba's own transfiguration by divine light.

After Columba's death, the influence of Iona spread into northern England, most notably when St Aidan was sent from Iona as a missionary bishop at the request of King Oswald of Northumbria, who had become a Christian while in exile on Iona. Lindisfarne became an important outpost of Ionan influence, and from there Irish missionaries brought the Christian faith to Northumbria and to parts of East Anglia and the Midlands. The finest remaining monument to their influence may be seen in the beautiful Lindisfarne Gospels.

The second saint is no less significant. On 5 June 754, St Boniface was murdered while bringing the Christian faith to the impoverished tribes of fisherfolk who inhabited the North Sea islands of Frisia, now in Holland. A book of prayers that he was carrying still bears the marks of the axe that felled him: it is stained with his blood. Very shortly after his death, Boniface was acclaimed by the English Church as a martyr missionary on a par with St Augustine of Canterbury himself.

Boniface was born in Crediton in Devon. He was formed as a monk near Winchester, and went as a missionary priest to the Continent, where he worked for a time assisting St Willibrord, who was one of the first English missionaries. Later, Boniface went twice to Rome and was charged by the popes to bring Christianity as a missionary bishop to the

Saxons living to the east of the Rhine. We have a very full picture of his activities from his numerous letters that were addressed to the popes in Rome, to rulers in France and England, and to his supporters in the English Church. Boniface was in fact partly responsible for laying the foundation of the partnership between the Frankish monarchy and the papacy that was to have such a significant impact in European history. Boniface was an energetic reformer, who ruffled feathers among some of the Frankish bishops as he challenged problems and weaknesses in the life of their church. Meanwhile, he founded new dioceses east of the Rhine, creating a monastery at Fulda, where he now lies buried. He attracted others from England to the mission field, both men and women, and the German Church regards Boniface as its apostle.

Columba and Boniface embodied the spirit of Christian mission in and from these islands in a way that set a potent example to their own generations and to those that came after them. First, they took seriously the words of St Paul about being constrained by the love of Christ. They cared that people should know the love of God revealed in Jesus Christ. Second, they both believed that education was the key to effective evangelism—education embodied in books, but also by example. Neither Columba nor Boniface sought to compel belief, nor did Augustine of Canterbury; and this principle was upheld by Alcuin in confrontation with Charlemagne in the years after Boniface's death. Finally, their evangelism by word, deed and teaching was rooted in holiness of life. Their prayers were the wellspring of their spiritual life and influence, and their prayers—and their mission—were rooted in and sustained by their monastic communities.

This letter of St Boniface, written in 738 to friends back in England, captures the spirit of his mission:

> We beg you, brethren, out of love for us to remember us in your prayers, that we may escape the opposition of the enemy and all the assaults of evil men, so that the word of God may go forward and take root. We urge you to carry on praying that God and our Lord Jesus Christ, who desire the salvation of all by the knowledge of the Trinity, may convert the hearts of the heathen Saxons to Christianity. May they reject the errors of paganism

and become true children of the Church our mother. Take pity upon them, for they often say to us: "We are of the same flesh and blood as you!" For this work I have received the encouragement and active support of two bishops of the Holy See of Rome. Please respond to my request for prayer, so that your reward in heaven may be great in the presence of God's holy angels. So may God the Almighty Creator preserve you in unity and in the fellowship of his love forever.

5 4

St Benedict

11 July

Whenever we say the words, "O God, make speed to save us: O Lord, make haste to help us," at the beginning of prayers in church, we share in the way in which Benedictine monasticism has shaped the English Church from the beginning. These words come from the opening of Psalm 70 and St Benedict commanded their use each time psalms were recited. They encapsulate an inner prayer of dependence and devotion towards God, linking private prayer to public worship by the daily recitation of the psalms. Clergy are still expected to recite the full psalter each month, as can be seen in the lay-out of the psalms in the *Book of Common Prayer*. Rather like the Jesus Prayer in the Orthodox tradition, the prayer "O God, make speed to save us: O Lord, make haste to help us" can be used as a rhythmic meditation, perhaps linked to breathing, that speaks from the heart, but which is also an instrument of contemplative intercession for others.

Benedict lived in Italy in the sixth century and died around the year 550. His life was written up a generation later by St Gregory the Great, and it was his authority as pope that commended the *Life of Benedict* and his *Rule of St Benedict* to the later medieval Church. Gregory was himself a monk and his *Life of St Benedict* is the principal source for information about the saint. Benedict was born in Nursia and educated in Rome, whence he departed to live the life of a hermit in the mountains at Subiaco. He was soon joined by others, though not without dissension, which caused him to remove to Monte Cassino, where he wrote his *Rule*. This distilled the wisdom of earlier monastic traditions, Eastern and Western, and it remains an outstanding work of moderation and wisdom in the pursuit of the spiritual life and the organization of Christian life in community. Its influence has stretched far and wide beyond the confines of monastic life.

We know from the writings of Bede that the *Life* and the *Rule of St Benedict* penetrated and influenced him and the early Anglo-Saxon Church. One of the first English bishops, Wilfrid, commanded use of the *Rule*, and Benedict Biscop, the founder of the monastery where Bede grew up and worked, also commended it. Willibrord and Boniface promoted its use on the Continent, while Alcuin was active in promoting the teaching and example of Benedictine monasticism there, which took formal shape early in the ninth century under the leadership of his younger contemporary and friend, Benedict of Aniane. By the tenth century, the revival of monasticism on the Continent and in England was firmly Benedictine in its ethos, most notably at Cluny. Fleury became the centre of the cult of Benedict in northern Europe, claiming his relics; and in England the *Regularis Concordia* drawn up at Winchester by Dunstan and Ethelwold around the year 970 wove together the demands of the *Rule of St Benedict* with local customs in the English Church. Perhaps the most striking development at this time in England was that of monk-bishops, like Dunstan, Ethelwold and Oswald, living within a monastic community based at a cathedral. Central to this whole development, from the time of Bede through that of Alcuin and into the tenth century, was Christian learning and education, not something envisaged in the original *Rule of St Benedict*, but highly influential in its impact in England and on the Continent. The oldest manuscript of the *Rule of St Benedict* now remaining was actually written in England around the year 700: it is in the Bodleian Library in Oxford.

What is distinctive about the ethos of Benedictine monasticism as enshrined in the *Rule of St Benedict*? Its prologue opens with these famous words: "Listen, my son, to the precepts of a master and incline the ear of your heart: willingly receive and faithfully fulfil the admonition of a loving father; so that you may return by the labour of obedience to him from you departed through the laziness of disobedience." Behind these words stands the parable of the Prodigal Son. The divine summons to return is personal, and life in a monastery provides a secure and stable way back to God our loving heavenly Father, whose authority is to be exercised by the abbot himself. Life in a monastery is therefore rather like being in the army—under willing obedience to become equipped for a spiritual fight that will last a lifetime. As in the army, however, no-one fights alone: the monastic community is like a regiment, with each person allotted tasks and duties under obedience; effective leadership of such a community is of crucial importance.

Close attention to the actual words from the prologue of the *Rule of St Benedict* discloses some of its deeper meaning, in ways comparable with the words of Scripture. Note the appeal is personal, and to "listen"—not just once but every day. This implies a steady willingness to learn, to take responsibility and, if need be, to repent. The "ear of the heart" is a biblical phrase, evident in the psalms. It signifies a deep and willing response to the call of God to each person: "Adam, where are you?" Life in a monastery is therefore a lifetime commitment to reformation, a process of divine remaking. It also entails a spiritual education that requires diligent seeking, serious and disciplined attention, and willing assent. It is not about dragooning people or indoctrinating them by an authoritarian regime. The twin pillars of monastic life, as indeed of all Christian life, are faithfulness and obedience. As in a marriage, human faithfulness is called to mirror and to express the faithfulness of God revealed in Jesus Christ. Likewise, Christian obedience is never mere subservience, but rather loving sensitivity to the needs and demands of others, including superiors, as towards God himself. In the words of Jesus, "Insofar as you cared for the least of these my brethren, you cared for me" (Matthew 25:40). In a monastery, every person is a brother or sister, and every guest is a child of God, and therefore Benedict said in his *Rule*, "Let the visitor be welcomed as Christ himself."

The *Rule of St Benedict*, like the *Pastoral Care* of Gregory the Great, addresses how authority is to be exercised within the life of the Church or of any Christian community. This is why its influence has spread far and wide: its wisdom and moderation make it perfectly adaptable to running schools and other organizations. The abbot is commanded to remember the source and nature of his authority, for the word "authority" implies something essentially life-giving to enable others to function and to flourish. The abbot is also accountable directly to Christ for his conduct as a good shepherd: "Therefore the abbot should never teach, enact or command anything contrary to the precepts of the Lord... Let equal love be shown to all." The abbot is to be adaptable, "mingling gentleness with sternness, alternating the strictness of a master with the loving affection shown by a father". Everyone is to participate openly in all decisions "because it is often to the younger person that the Lord reveals what is best"; and examples of this occur in the Bible.

What picture of Benedict himself emerges from the *Life of St Benedict* that Gregory included within his *Dialogues*? There is no doubt that how Gregory portrayed the saint deeply influenced later hagiography throughout the Middle Ages. Perhaps the most famous and striking story in the *Life of St Benedict* is this one:

> When the brothers were still asleep, the man of God, Benedict, got up to watch in prayer before the time for the Night Office. Standing at the window and praying to Almighty God in the middle of the night, he suddenly saw a light pour down that routed all the shadows. It shone with such splendour that it surpassed day-light, even though it was shining in the darkness. A wonderful thing followed in this vision, for as Benedict reported later, the whole world was brought before his eyes as if collected in a single ray of sunlight.

The comment of Gregory about this is no less significant: "To a person who sees the Creator, every creature looks narrow by comparison... for the capacity of the mind is expanded by the light of inner contemplation ... and the soul becomes greater than itself through contemplation.... Swept up into God, it can easily see whatever is beneath God."

It was through the spiritual genius of Benedict and Gregory that so stable a ladder of divine ascent was created within the life of the Western Church that has lasted to this day. Benedict is regarded as the Patriarch of Western Monasticism and a Patron of European Christianity.

5 5

St James the Apostle

Acts 12; 2 Corinthians 4:7–15; Matthew 20:20–8

On 25 July, the Church keeps the feast of St James the Apostle, the brother of John, both of whom were sons of Zebedee and initially fishermen in Galilee (Mark 1:19). With Peter, they were key witnesses of the raising of Jairus' daughter by Jesus, the Transfiguration of the Lord, and of his agony in the Garden of Gethsemane. Jesus called them "the Sons of Thunder" because of their zeal and strength of character (Mark 3:17). James was the first of the twelve apostles to be martyred, by Herod in AD 44 (Acts 12:2). Many centuries later, it was believed that his body was conveyed to Santiago de Compostela in Spain, where there is a major shrine in his honour which has become a great centre of pilgrimage. James the Apostle is not to be confused with James the Lord's brother, who became the leader of the church in Jerusalem (Galatians 1:19), and to whom Jesus appeared personally after his resurrection (1 Corinthians 15:7). It is believed that he was killed on the orders of the Sanhedrin in Jerusalem in AD 62, and his memory remained important for Jewish Christians for many centuries thereafter. There is another James among the twelve disciples in the Gospels, nicknamed 'the Little' (Mark 15:40), who may be the same person as James, the son of Alphaeus (Mark 3:18). He is commemorated with his fellow apostle Philip on 1 May. Today, historically, the feast of St Peter in Chains commemorates his miraculous escape from prison as recorded in Acts 12 shortly after the murder of James by Herod.

How did the earliest Christians anticipate and understand martyrdom, which was already part of the experience of their fellow Jews? Fundamentally, of course, this was the consequence of defying foreign political authority, Greek or Roman, which sought to crush independent religious practice. By modern standards, Jewish and Christian martyrdom was in defence of the basic human right to freedom of worship and to express religious belief. It is notable that there is no evidence of Christians resorting to violence in self-defence, as the Jewish Zealots did at Masada, for example, after the fall of Jerusalem in AD 70. Christians were articulate, however, in their non-violent resistance to persecution, whether by Jewish or Roman authorities; and in the fourth century, under Constantine, persecution of Christianity was stopped within the Roman Empire.

"Are you able to drink the cup that I am about to drink?" These challenging words of Jesus to James and John, when their mother was trying to secure their promotion in the kingdom of God (Matthew 20:22), provide a powerful clue to what is distinctive about Christian martyrdom, then and subsequently. The word "martyr" means "witness"—but in this case to the death and resurrection of Jesus himself. In the book of Revelation, the seer sees "underneath the altar (of heaven) the souls of them that had been slain for the Word of God and for the testimony that they held" (Revelation 6:9). These are they "who overcame evil because of the blood of the Lamb and the word of their testimony, for they loved not their life even unto death" (Revelation 12:11). The Greek word used here for "testimony" is *martyrion*, and in many ways the book of Revelation is a great monument to the martyrdom of early Christians. Martyrdom is essentially conflict with evil itself in the power of the crucified Christ.

It is Paul who gives us an insight into how Christians anticipated and experienced martyrdom, and his most significant testimony is in 2 Corinthians. His ministry and mission were under continuous pressure and danger, and this is evident in the Acts of the Apostles: "Pressed in on every side but not squashed, often perplexed but not in despair, pursued but never forsaken, struck down but not yet destroyed" (2 Corinthians 4:8–9). Paul did not believe in success, nor did he think that Christian evangelism was an advertising programme that could be delivered with sure results. Rather, it was his sufferings that signified to him and to others the redeeming work of Christ among his hearers.

His own testimony here is very striking: "We are always bearing about in the body the dying of Jesus, that the life of Jesus may be manifested in our mortal flesh. So then, death works in us, but life in you" (2 Corinthians 4:10-12). In Greek, the phrase "the dying of Jesus" means experiencing something of how Jesus was himself put to death. The Gospels show us that his whole ministry was persecuted in various ways from its inception and his was a path of "living through dying" to which Paul was also called. This means that Christian martyrdom in some way brings the mystery of the Lord's suffering and passion very close. The death of a martyr opens the door to the reality of the resurrection, for this is God's way of overcoming evil in the world and in the hearts of human beings.

The most vivid portrayal of this dynamic mystery is found in the account of the martyrdom of Polycarp, who died around the year AD 155. After refusing to be nailed to the stake, and having delivered a momentous prayer, this aged Christian bishop was roasted alive. "As a mighty flame blazed up, we saw a miracle ... for the fire, taking the shape of an arch, or like the sail of a ship filled by the wind, completely surrounded the body of the martyr; and he was there in the middle of the fire, not like flesh burning but rather like bread baking, or like gold and silver being refined in a furnace. For we perceived also a very fragrant aroma, as if it were the scent of incense or some other precious spice."

Once again, the testimony of Paul is potent: "Thanks be to God who always leads us as captives in Christ's triumphal procession, and uses us to spread abroad the fragrance of the knowledge of himself. We are indeed incense offered by Christ to God, both among those who are on the way to salvation, and among those on the way to destruction. To the latter this is a deadly fume that kills, but to the former it is a vital fragrance that brings life. Who can be equal to such a calling?" (2 Corinthians 2:14-16).

Yet some are equal to such a calling in every generation of the Church, for its roots and its life lie in martyrdom, and "the blood of the martyrs is the seed of the Church" (Tertullian). It is hard for those living in England, with no significant experience of martyrdom in the formation of the Church here, to fathom the mystery of Christian martyrdom, its horror and its transforming joy. Across the world today, however, and in too many places, Christians are being martyred for their faith, being denied jobs, homes, education and basic freedoms. Their suffering stands alongside all those being persecuted for their identity and faith.

To commemorate a martyr in the life of the Church is to affirm the bond of love and concern that unites all Christians, something which brings comfort to those who are under persecution now, and also puts pressure on their persecutors. Their plight must never be forgotten in our prayers, and their cause needs to be publicized and upheld in a free and open society.

5 6

Jesu Dulcis Memoria

Remembering St Bernard of Clairvaux

The feast of St Bernard of Clairvaux falls on 20 August: he was born around the year 1090 and died in 1153. As a young man of noble background, born near Dijon in France, Bernard, aged 22, led a group of like-minded friends to become monks at Citeaux, which was a destitute monastery in Burgundy. Soon after this arduous beginning, Bernard became Abbot of Clairvaux, which he founded in 1115. By the time of his death, Clairvaux numbered more than 700 monks, having served as the impetus and model for the foundation of 500 Cistercian monasteries across Europe, including several in England, notably at Rievaulx in Yorkshire, which was founded in 1132.

The Cistercians sought to follow the *Rule of St Benedict* more strictly, with less elaborate ritual and artistry in church. Many of the loveliest Romanesque churches of the twelfth century were built by Cistercians as their order spread far and wide, often leading the way in economic development and organization. Bernard himself became a notable churchman of great influence, which reached its peak when a disciple of his became Pope Eugenius III in 1145. Bernard challenged some of the intellectual developments in theology in Paris and elsewhere, and became an ardent propagandist for the Second Crusade, which ended in disaster.

Bernard was a great preacher and a person of charismatic influence, revered by many, feared by some, and bitterly opposed by his critics. Yet in the midst of so active and articulate a public role, Bernard managed to give voice to some of the deepest and most beautiful mystical theology, expounding the inner life of prayer, and illuminating the presence of the love of God within the human heart in a way that has never been surpassed. His influence on the Franciscans in the thirteenth century was profound.

The beautiful Latin hymn *Jesu Dulcis Memoria* dates from the twelfth century, being probably composed not by Bernard himself, but perhaps by an unknown Cistercian in England. Its ethos expresses well the vision of Jesus that inspired Bernard and those who followed his teaching and example. In his classic spiritual masterpiece *On the Love of God*, Bernard said this: "When I name Jesus, I set before me someone meek and lowly of heart, kind, sober, chaste, merciful, and adorned with all grace and holiness; but at the same time, God's own self, the Almighty, who makes me whole by his own example and strong by his help." Devotion to the holy Name of Jesus emerged from Cistercian piety as personal prayer to someone who may be addressed directly and with fervent love.

Jesu Dulcis Memoria is translated in several hymns that are used today, notably "Jesu, the very thought of thee" and "Jesu, thou joy of loving hearts". These make a very immediate way into the spiritual theology of Bernard and the Cistercians. These lovely words plunge us deep into the love that can arise in the human heart when a person draws near to Jesus in prayer and worship. In the Gospel, Jesus said to his disciples: "I have called you friends, and you are my friends if you do what I command you" (John 15:14–15). Careful reading of the Gospel reveals how Jesus related to his friends, most strikingly perhaps to Mary Magdalene, Thomas and Peter after his resurrection. Friendship with Jesus is at the heart of Christian experience.

The words of these moving hymns in translation lead us back to the Gospel and the promise of Jesus of the gift of himself in the midst of controversy and conflict arising from misunderstanding and hostility. The bread of life that he gives is his own flesh, given for the life of the world. Only by embracing the suffering love of Jesus as it is given to us in the sacrament of Holy Communion do we come to abide in him and he in us. We have to seek this with our whole heart—to seek Jesus with the same love with which he seeks us.

There are times when to follow Jesus is to enter darkness, moments when his smile seems only a distant memory. Then we must cling on to our faith in his holy Name: "for there is salvation in no other person, nor is there any other name under heaven given to human beings whereby we must be saved" (Acts 4:12). Peter professed belief in Jesus as "the Holy One of God" (John 6:69), but went on to deny Jesus in a moment of panic, before he could proclaim the universal significance of the saving name of his Lord before the priests in Jerusalem.

The lovely hymn *Jesu Dulcis Memoria* draws us close to the feet of Jesus and to his warm embrace of us as his friends. But it also reminds us of the cost of that friendship, to him and also to us. It warns us against complacency or sentimentality, or making an image of Jesus which is not rooted in the truth of the Gospels. Devotion to the holy Name of Jesus is not a cult but love towards a living and loving person, as in the words of the Jesus Prayer: "Lord Jesus Christ, Son of the Living God, have mercy upon me, a sinner." The strength and wisdom of this ancient prayer is that its words spring from the Gospels, from actual encounters that people had with Jesus, by which they were saved; and many of them became his friends.

The words of the Jesus Prayer used together with those of the hymn *Jesu Dulcis Memoria* safeguard our inner life of personal prayer by preparing us for the gift of Jesus himself in Holy Communion. They challenge us with the personal call of Jesus to each one of us: "What do you really want? Do you want to be made whole? Then follow me!" We only receive communion after hearing his awesome words: "This is my Body that is given up for you ... This is my blood which is shed for you." Then we may make Peter's words our own: "Lord, to whom shall we go? You have the words of eternal life. We believe and know that you are indeed the Holy One of God."

57

Amor Vincit Omnia

A sermon for the feast of St Augustine of Hippo

The feast of St Augustine of Hippo is kept on 28 August. His importance for the history of the Western Church is of the greatest significance, as his theological writings formed the belief of the Middle Ages and also exercised great influence at the Reformation. Indeed, the most accessible witness to his spiritual legacy is to be found in the collects of the *Book of Common Prayer*.

Augustine was born in North Africa in 354 and grew up in Carthage. His father was nominally a Christian, while his mother, Monica, was more devout. He trained in Rome as a legal advocate before moving to Milan, where he came under the influence of St Ambrose, who was then the bishop there. In his *Confessions*, Augustine recounts his spiritual journey into Christian faith. His was the first Christian autobiographical writing since that of St Paul in 2 Corinthians and Philippians.

He writes about his childhood and adolescence, and his half-hearted search for truth during his education. In due time, he fell in with the cult of the Manichees, while also reading the writings of some Greek and Roman philosophers. No-one could answer his questions. Finally, and perhaps somewhat reluctantly, he became a Christian and was baptized in 386 in Milan. He recounts how the voice of a child playing a game nearby with the tag, *Tolle—Lege*, which means "pick it up and read it!", prompted him to open St Paul's letter to the Romans, where a particular verse (13:13–14) seemed to address him directly and to pierce his heart. He remembered the story of how St Anthony had begun his own Christian path as a monk in Egypt in exactly the same way, prompted by the Gospel of the day. Augustine says, "I had no wish to read more and no need to do so. For in an instant, as I finished the sentence, it was as though the light of confidence flooded into my heart, and all the darkness of my doubt was swept away."

He returned to North Africa, where he was ordained a priest in 391, and by 396 was Bishop of Hippo, a port on the coast, where he remained until his death 34 years later in 430. By then, the world that he had grown up in was changing fast as the Western Roman Empire crumbled; and Augustine died while the Vandals were besieging his city. He had an eventful career as a bishop and left a vast body of writings, some of which he revised towards the end of his life.

Most notable are the *Confessions* themselves, and his extensive *Homilies* on the Gospel of John and on the Psalms, which were noted down as he delivered them in church. Also, his *De Trinitate*, which comprises a searching consideration of the heart of Christian belief about God; and *The City of God*, a wide-ranging discussion of the ways of God in human history, prompted by the sack of Rome in 410, and the significance and true nature of the Church as safeguarding the true purpose and destiny of human life.

St Augustine was a person of genius, who possessed one of the finest minds that has ever attempted to communicate Christian belief. A way to capture the essence of his thought and vision is to reflect on these short extracts from his writings:

> Give me chastity, Lord, but not yet.

This frank statement encapsulates the inner turmoil that beset Augustine's life as a young man. He knew how he ought to behave but was reluctant to give up a hedonistic way of life, especially after he settled down with a mistress by whom he had a son. In the end, he relinquished them both and never married. But his dilemma was deeper than sexual. He knew that human life is profoundly flawed, driven by passions that few can ever control for long. The unruly will and affections that express this unhappy truth nagged him throughout his life. Without divine grace and assistance, Augustine did not think that human beings stood a chance of becoming once again truly the children of God.

> Our hearts are restless until they find their rest in Thee.

Augustine recognized from his own experience how easily the human heart seeks fulfilment in things and people around it. "Our hearts are restless" ... His own emotional temperament is apparent in all that he wrote, as he wrestled with the meaning of Christian repentance and the hope of the restoration of inner integrity without which human life is meaningless and unhappy. Only God the Creator can re-create human beings in his own Image and Likeness, which was revealed once for all in the coming of Christ, the Word of God.

> Late have I loved Thee, Beauty so ancient and so new.

These moving words convey the deeply artistic and musical temperament of Augustine; and the latter part of the *Confessions* contains some of his most wondering writing about the mystery of creation, and the meaning of divine beauty which permeates all that we see. Intellectual though he certainly was, he was also a person whose heart was deeply moved. He sought love, and found it ultimately in the generous outpouring of the heart of God revealed in Jesus and made real by the indwelling of the Holy Spirit.

> Let God love himself through you.

These thought-provoking words challenge how we pray. St Paul speaks about the Spirit praying alongside and within us (Romans 8:26). Augustine gave to the Middle Ages the language of loving prayer, of intimacy with God, of life-long searching after the Beloved. His own reflections on the mystery of the Trinity led him to discern within a human person the triad of memory, intellect and will. This he perceived to be a reflection of the unity of God the Trinity, an inkling of how human beings are indeed made in the divine image and likeness. For, "since the time when I learned of you, you have always been present in my memory". Augustine's *Confessions* are a sustained prayer to God, modelled in part on the language of the Psalms. The word "confession" means both repentance and thanksgiving, both of which find their supreme expression in the Eucharist itself.

> In Thy Light do we see Light.

These words come from a psalm in the Old Testament (36:9) and they provide the catalyst for one of the most important legacies of Augustine to subsequent Christian thought. Just as we only see the manifold beauty of the created world with its rich diversity of colours in the invisible light of the sun, so we only understand the truth about spiritual reality within and beyond us by the light of God himself, which enables us to see anything truly at all. For Christ the Word of God is "the true light which enlightens everyone coming into the world" (John 1:9). Augustine believed that divine light enables human understanding. How otherwise could we know anything for certain, and how could we discern what is beautiful and good and true?

> In resting we see, in seeing we love, and in loving we praise,
> in the end that is no end.

Augustine once described heaven as "the homeland of the soul". His own reflections led him to value the mystery of the soul that is hidden in the deep heart of every human person. What is the destiny of human beings? Why are they made in the way that they are? How do they discover who they truly are? How may they come to know and love God, who is beyond their imagining? St Bernard of Clairvaux, who lived in the twelfth century, was deeply influenced by Augustine when he said: "Life is given to us that we may learn how to love; and time is given to us that we may find God."

In fact, it is God who seeks and finds us first, as these words of Augustine in the *Confessions* declare:

> You called and cried aloud to me—for you were within me. You broke the barrier of my deafness. You shone upon me. Your radiance enveloped me. You put my blindness to flight. You shed your fragrance about me. I drew in my breath, and now I gasp

for your sweet fragrance. I tasted you, and now I hunger and thirst for you. You touched me, and I am inflamed with the love of your peace.

5 8

Glory Transformed

*A meditation for the feast of the Nativity of the
Blessed Virgin Mary—8 September*

> They are Israelites, whose are the Adoption as sons, the Glory, the Covenants, the giving of the Law, the Worship of God, and the Promises; whose also are the Fathers: and of whom is Christ, born in the flesh, who is over all, God blessed forever.
>
> *Romans 9:4–5*

Today, as we celebrate the birth of the Blessed Virgin Mary, we give thanks for her life-giving obedience and humility as the holy Mother of our Lord, the *Theotokos*. Every time we salute her, we affirm her as the epitome of the faithfulness of Israel. In her was brought to an intense focus all that this text in Romans conveys about the singular and historical vocation of God's people, Israel. The poetry that surrounds St Luke's account of the Annunciation and the birth of Jesus—the *Magnificat*, the *Benedictus* and the *Nunc Dimittis*—all conveys the same message. Mary was nurtured in a devout and loving family, where worship was central, and meditation on Scripture was formative of her thought. The *Magnificat* is her witness to this rich inheritance. For Mary is the historical and human context for the coming of Jesus the Messiah. As she holds him on her lap, she affirms this vital truth, just as she points us to her first-born son, whom we are called to cherish and to serve with all our heart.

In Jesus Christ, all the rich inheritance of Israel was fulfilled and transformed, and never set aside, as Paul affirms in his letter to the Romans. As the only Son of God, he makes us the children of God by adoption and grace. In his transfigured face, the glory of God shines forth in human form, as the true Image and Likeness of God. Jesus fulfils the redeeming covenants and promises of God; and he is the living Law of God, to whom Moses and Elijah bore witness on the holy mountain of Transfiguration. He is also "the Word made flesh"—vulnerable human flesh in which he suffered and died on the Cross of Calvary. In this way, he revealed how divine love overcomes evil and eradicates sin, pouring forgiveness and new life into human hearts, and also into the world of God's creation, "destroying death by death".

Through the lens of the Incarnation, and uniquely in the faithfulness of Mary and Jesus himself, is focused the whole loving purpose of God, Father, Son and Holy Spirit, whose goal is this: "Christ in you—the hope of glory" (Colossians 1:27). Our vocation is to welcome him into our hearts, making the prayer of Mary our own: "*Fiat mihi, Domine, secundum verbum Tuum*—May it be unto me according to your word" (Luke 1:38). When we do this, we become truly the children of God, united with Christ in his love and obedience to the Father. If we welcome the Holy Spirit of Christ into our lives, his glory will shine forth in hidden but life-giving ways, transforming us into the likeness of Christ. Our humble faithfulness will reflect and express the faithfulness of God, whose promises never fail. If our lives are ruled by the law of divine love, we shall stand on the threshold of the worship of heaven in communion with all those who have gone before us, and whose worship now sustains and deepens our own. As we receive the holy gift of the Eucharist, we receive the kiss of his peace and love in the words, "The Body and Blood of Christ that is given for you."

St Bonaventure summed up our vocation as Christians in these lovely words: "What then remains to be done? Only this—to carry the Son of God and the Son of the Virgin Mary to the heavenly Jerusalem and into the Temple of God, and there present him to the Father." Let us embrace the loving humility of God in the person of Jesus, "whose power is stronger, whose generosity more abundant, whose appearance is more beautiful, whose courtesy more gracious; and in whose embrace, you are already caught up: for you are the spouse, the mother and the sister of our Lord Jesus Christ". St Clare goes on to bid us to "be strengthened in the holy service which you have undertaken out of ardent desire for the Poor Crucified One". St Bonaventure says elsewhere that "so great a love longs for and craves for your heart; such love longs to embrace you. Jesus cries out, saying, 'The reason I became visible was in order that you might see me and give me your love. I gave myself to you: will you give yourself to me?'" Let us say with all our heart, and in union with the prayer of holy Mary herself, "Behold, I am the handmaid of the Lord: may it be to me according to your word." Amen.

59

The Song of Creation

Remembering St Francis of Assisi

St Francis of Assisi died on 4 October 1226 at the age of 44 and was declared a saint two years later by Pope Gregory IX. Although he rapidly became a legendary figure, it is quite possible to appreciate directly the heart of his spiritual teaching from his writings that remain. One of the most compelling of these is his famous *Canticle of Brother Sun*, which forms the basis for a well-loved hymn—"All creatures of our God and King". The original version was composed by Francis on three occasions towards the end of his life, and after he had received the stigmata at La Verna.

Francis said this about its initial composition: "For his praise, I wish to compose a new hymn about the Lord's creatures, of which we make daily use, without which we cannot live, and with which the human race greatly offends its Creator." The second part of the hymn was composed to bring about peace among quarrelling factions in Assisi. The last part was composed as Francis was anticipating his own death. As a hymn about creation, it has its antecedents in the Bible, most notably in the Song of the Three Young Jewish Men thrown into the fiery furnace for their faith, as recorded in Daniel 3. In the Greek text of Daniel, a great canticle of praise is recorded that they sang while standing in the midst of the fire, from which they emerged unscathed. It is called *Benedicite Omnia Opera* and is found in the *Book of Common Prayer* as well as in *Common Worship*. The text of the hymn composed by Francis is important also as a witness to the emergence of Italian from Latin. Later legends about Francis record his profound love of the natural world and his affinity with birds and animals, even preaching to them!

The reason that Francis gave for composing this hymn remains strikingly relevant as the celebration of harvest each year is now so closely linked to how we value and use, or misuse, the created world. Firstly, it recognizes that every aspect of creation is the handiwork of God and his gift to the human race. Secondly, it reminds us that our life utterly depends upon a stable natural order, which we should never take for granted. Thirdly, it exposes and condemns the abuse of the natural world that was already taking place in the thirteenth century, and has reached a crescendo in our own time. Instead, Francis demonstrated a profound affinity with and sensitivity to other creatures, whom he addressed as his brethren. It is too easy to sentimentalize the memory and example of Francis and to turn him into a symbol for various ecological causes.

The key to understanding exactly what he was saying and why he said it in this hymn is found in this explanation by St Bonaventure in his *Life of Francis*, for Francis and Bonaventure regarded the created world as a living icon of God's glory:

> Aroused by all things to the love of God, Francis rejoiced in all the works of the Lord's hands; and from these joyful manifestations he rose to their life-giving Principle and Cause—God himself. In such beautiful things he saw Divine Beauty itself; and through his finger-prints imprinted upon creation, Francis followed his Beloved everywhere, making everything a ladder by which he could climb up and embrace him who is utterly desirable.

Each aspect of creation became for Francis an intimate window into the reality and glory of God, who is praised by him in words that echo the hymns in the book of Revelation: "Most High, all-powerful, good Lord: yours is the praise, the glory, the honour and all blessing!" First and foremost, the sun is invoked as "Sir Brother Sun", "who is the day and through whom you give us light. He is beautiful and radiant with great splendour; and he bears a likeness of You, Most High One." Only in the light of the sun can we see anything in all its beauty and detail; so, in the words of the Psalmist addressing God, "with You is the well of life, and in Your light, we see light" (Psalm 36:9).

All other parts of creation became for Francis the cause of thanksgiving, a means by which God can be praised, and a window into his continuing presence at the heart of creation. In this insight, Francis was clearly influenced by the language of the psalms, which he knew by heart: "Praise be You, my Lord, through Sister Moon and the stars: in heaven you formed them clear and precious and beautiful." The reflected light of the moon became for Bonaventure a clue to the nature of the Church, something that should be "clear, precious and beautiful". Today, we know that the stars shine with ancient light that originated long ago, and which comes to us even as they rush away from us into the vastness of the universe; potent signs indeed of the greatness of God the Creator.

"Praise be to You, O Lord, through Brother Wind, and through the air, so cloudy and serene; and through every kind of weather through which you give life to your creatures." It is an extraordinary and shocking achievement of modern society that its impact is now causing widespread climate change. Francis acclaimed water itself, the means of life, as "very useful, humble, precious and chaste", words that he also used to describe the vocation of his brothers and sisters. The word "humble" is an important clue to his thought and teaching, as it means "down to earth" by being rooted in honest recognition of the fragile reality of all created existence, including that of human beings, made "from the dust of the earth" (Genesis 2:7).

Fire itself mirrors the dynamic creativity of God; it "lights the night and is beautiful, playful, robust and so strong". Francis addressed Mother Earth as "our sister who sustains and governs us, producing varied fruits with brilliant and colourful flowers and herbs". His vision of the earth was of a place of beauty and life, designed for human collaboration with the natural order rather than exploitation and manipulation of it. Francis knew from his own experience how easily the exploitation of nature leads to the exploitation of human nature, as he and his brethren worked in the slums on the edge of rapidly growing cities in Italy and elsewhere in the thirteenth century. His vision of the natural world was quickly taken up by the artist Giotto as he decorated the great basilica in Assisi where Francis is now buried. Giotto and later Masaccio saw the world of nature and of human nature with new eyes.

The second part of the hymn is a direct appeal for human repentance and forgiveness: "Praise be to You, through those who show forgiveness in response to Your love, bearing infirmity and tribulation. How blessed are those who endure in peace, for they will be crowned by You." These words directly echo those of Jesus himself in the Beatitudes. They also encapsulate the ethos of the Franciscan way, rooted in the humble but fearless example and teaching of Francis himself, and also of St Clare.

The last part of the hymn addresses Death itself as a welcome sister to bring us to God. "Praise be to you, O Lord, through our sister Death from whom no living person can escape . . . Blessed are those whom Death will find enfolded within Your most holy will." At the end of his life, as he lay dying, Francis reminded his brethren not to assume anything in the face of death, saying, "Let us begin, brothers, to serve the Lord our God: for up to now we have made little or no progress." The closing words of his great hymn gave them, as they give us, a proper sense of values and direction: "Praise and bless the Lord and give him thanks; and serve him with great humility."

The ecological crisis of our day has its roots in human sinfulness and wilful disregard for God; and without deep inner repentance it will not be effectively addressed. Harvest reminds us each year that created life is the gift of God, and that the created world is not our possession, but rather a solemn trust for the use of which we will each have to give an account. This is why thanksgiving in the Eucharist each week expresses the heart of the Church's life and worship and vision, being the wellspring of Christian values, and our heartfelt response to God the Giver of Good.

60

A Martyr King

The significance of King Edmund the Martyr

For English Christians, the annual feast of Christ the King on the last Sunday before Advent is anchored in the memory of the grim challenge faced by an early English ruler, who chose to follow the non-violent example of Jesus in the Gospels. Edmund was king of East Anglia in the ninth century, and he was confronted by a Viking invasion in 869. The Viking leader offered him his life if he would collaborate with him. Edmund refused to do this as it would subject his people to slavery; and for this refusal he was brutally murdered. His feast day falls on 20 November.

The story of what happened to King Edmund rests upon a secure line of transmission, for St Dunstan heard it many years later as a young man at the court of King Athelstan from the elderly shield-bearer of the murdered king. Towards the end of his life in 985, Dunstan, as Archbishop of Canterbury, briefed his friend Abbo, a visiting Frankish scholar from Fleury, who composed a Latin *Life of St Edmund*, which was then carefully translated into English by a leading monastic scholar at Winchester called Aelfric. Here is Aelfric's account of what happened to King Edmund in his homily for the feast of the martyred king:

> The Viking lord, Hingwar, sent messengers to king Edmund of East Anglia demanding that he surrender his people into captivity in return for his own life. The king replied, "It was never my custom to flee, and I would rather die if I must for my own land and people. For I will never turn aside from the worship of Almighty God, and that Hingwar knows well; nor will I betray

my love of him for life or death." Edmund then turned to the messenger: "Say this to your cruel lord, that Edmund the king will never bow in this life to Hingwar the heathen leader, unless he will first bow in my land and in true faith to Jesus Christ.

When he heard this, Hingwar commanded that his forces should first secure the king alone, who had thus despised him. Edmund met him, standing in his hall without weapons, remembering the example of Christ, who had forbidden Peter to fight back with force. They seized and bound the king and tied him to a tree. They scourged him with whips while he called on Christ to help him. Then they shot arrows at him for their amusement. Finally, when Hingwar realized that Edmund would never deny Christ, but still called upon him faithfully, he cut off his head. His soul thus escaped joyfully to Christ, his beloved Lord.

Aelfric's translation of the *Life of St Edmund* reveals a great deal about the king's reputation as a ruler. He took to heart explicitly the teaching of Christ that "if you are chief do not exalt yourself, but be among your people as one of them". He was generous to the poor and widows as a true father of his people, while being firm with the violent and unjust. Hingwar by contrast was ruthless, "stalking the land like a wolf and killing men, women and innocent children, shamefully tormenting Christians".

The bishops do not come out of this story very well, as the one closest to Edmund advised surrender and flight. The king reproved him: "The poor people of this land are brought to shame, and it is now dearer to me that I should fall in the fight against him who would take possession of my people's inheritance. I cannot be left safe and alone after my supporters have been slain in their beds with their families by these seamen." This conversation apparently took place while the Viking messenger waited for a reply. Many years later, when Edmund's burial place had become a shrine, the then Bishop of London, Theodred, hung a group of men who tried to break in to steal its treasures. He later realized with remorse his error as a bishop in condemning men to death in this way, and "he ever deplored it to his life's end".

Edmund's murder proves the truth of the famous dictum of Tertullian in the second century, that "the blood of the martyrs is the seed of the Church". Local people rescued the mutilated body of their king and found his severed head being guarded by a wolf, which followed them tamely back to their town. They built a small church over Edmund's burial place, which was later enlarged in times of peace. When they came to translate his remains in 915, they found his body to be incorrupt, like those of St Cuthbert and St Etheldreda. Its wounds were healed "and so he lies incorrupt to this day", a healing symbol of the reality of the resurrection and the indwelling of the Holy Spirit.

King Athelstan later created a religious community there in 925, which became in due time the major Benedictine monastery of Bury St Edmunds at the behest of the Viking ruler Canute in 1020. Its authority was extended throughout much of Suffolk by King Edward the Confessor in 1044. The Normans rebuilt the church in 1095 and the feast of St Edmund became a prominent one throughout the English Church in the Middle Ages. The cathedral of Bury St Edmunds serves the diocese and people of Suffolk today.

At a more mundane level, but no less important, by the end of the ninth century silver coins were minted in London bearing the image of the martyred King Edmund. These were traded throughout East Anglia and elsewhere while the successors of Alfred the Great, as Christian kings, gradually extended their authority over the Danelaw. As a result of this policy of evangelization and accommodation of the Danish population, England had for a time in the tenth century an Archbishop of Canterbury called Oda, who was of Viking heritage, and then an Archbishop of York called Oskytel, also of Viking origin. Some of the most important Benedictine monasteries were founded in East Anglia in the time of St Dunstan after 960 with support from both English and Danish nobility, notably Ely, Peterborough, Thorney, Crowland and Ramsey. Missionaries of both races went from them to Scandinavia to advance the life of the Church in Sweden and Norway. The death of St Edmund proved fruitful indeed, and throughout the Middle Ages he was regarded and portrayed as a patron of England.

Aelfric concluded that Edmund's shrine should be venerated "because a saint is greater than people imagine. The English nation is not deprived of the Lord's saints, since in English soil lie such saints as this holy king, and also blessed Cuthbert, saint Etheldreda and also her sister in Ely, all of whom are incorrupt for the confirmation of Christian faith, along with many other saints among the English, who work many miracles as is widely known." For in the words of the Psalmist, "How dear in the Lord's sight is the death of his saints" (Psalm 116:15).

Other books by Douglas Dales

Living through Dying: The Spiritual Experience of St Paul

Dunstan: Saint and Statesman

*Light to the Isles: Mission and Theology in
Celtic and Anglo-Saxon Britain*

Alcuin: His Life and Legacy

Alcuin: Theology and Thought

Divine Remaking: St Bonaventure and the Gospel of Luke

Way Back to God: The Spiritual Theology of St Bonaventure

Truth & Reality: The Wisdom of St Bonaventure

This is my Faith: A Confirmation Book

Prayers of our Faith

A Mind Intent on God: The Prayers and Spiritual Writings of Alcuin

Glory: The Spiritual Theology of Michael Ramsey

Glory Descending: Michael Ramsey and His Writings

The Spring of Hope

EU GPSR Authorized Representative:

LOGOS EUROPE, 9 rue Nicolas Poussin, 17000 La Rochelle, France

contact@logoseurope.eu

www.ingramcontent.com/pod-product-compliance
Lightning Source LLC
Chambersburg PA
CBHW070548160426
43199CB00014B/2423